I0163411

"Wisdom That Transforms. Action That Lasts."

Our Commitment

We believe that true wisdom has the power to transform lives. Our mission is to equip readers with timeless insights and practical tools that inspire growth, guide decisions, and empower purposeful living. We don't just inform—we empower.

Our books combine profound understanding with real-life application, enabling readers to unlock their potential and navigate life's challenges with clarity and confidence. With each step guided by wisdom, we help you create lasting change and live the life you deserve.

When wisdom meets purpose, transformation follows.

Commit to your core values. They will drive your life!

Copyright

Choose Core Values: Build Your Life or Business on Ethical Principles and Honorable Character Traits, by J. S. Wellman, published by Extra-mile Publishing, Box 465, Thompsons Station, TN 37179, copyright © 2023, J. S. Wellman

ISBN 978-1-952359-68-2   (hardcover)
ISBN 978-1-952359-49-1   (paperback)
ISBN 978-1-952359-50-7   (kindle)
Audiobook Available   (Amazon.com and Audible.com)

This book is available as an audiobook on our Amazon Life Planning book series page:

Acknowledgments

My wife has patiently persevered while I indulged my interest in this subject. Thank you for your patience.

Our older daughter has been an invaluable resource. She has also graciously produced our website at www.lifeplanningtools.com

Our middle daughter designed all the covers for this series. We are very grateful for her help, talent and creativity.

For More Information
About the Life Planning Series:

www.lifeplanningtools.com

Commit to your core values. They will drive your life!

Life Planning Series
by J. S. Wellman

Choose
Core Values

Build Your Life or Business on Ethical Principles and Honorable Character Traits

J. S. Wellman

LIFE PLANNING SERIES
J.S. WELLMAN

Extra-mile Publishing

This book is available as an audiobook on our Amazon Life Planning book series page:

Table of Contents

Commit to your core values. They will drive your life!

New For Employers!

POWERFUL
Business Strategies

Implementing Core Values
For Business Success

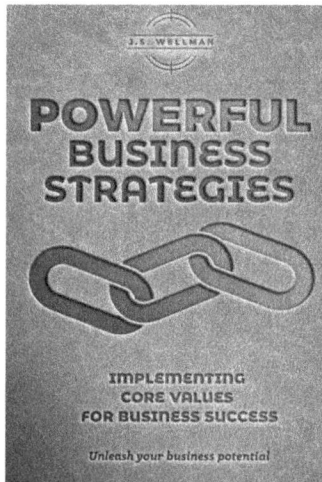

For your copy go to:
https://www.amazon.com/dp/1952359511

Message From the Author
Unlock Your Potential with Timeless Wisdom!

The general purpose of this book and the Life Planning Series is to encourage you to pursue actions and character traits that will produce your best life. The Series addresses ten different activities or traits that help people improve their lives, and *CHOOSE Core Values* addresses sixteen separate core values that you might consider beneficial.

Understand that you can improve or acquire high personal character and outstanding habits, no matter how good or bad your life may be at the moment. Good personal character <u>can be</u> achieved.

You don't have to read all the books in this series to make a significant change or improvement in your life. Find the books that focus on the areas of your life that you want to improve and dig in.

Know that this is a progressive journey. You may just want to learn more about the basic principles and concepts. This Series and this book will provide you with a foundation for decisions relative to your lifestyle, goals, priorities, and commitments.

The key to developing high character and making good decisions in your life is *intentionality*. The Life Planning Series will help you identify the path you want to travel but you will need to be intentional about walking that path. If you want to make progress toward the goal of living a better life, you must intentionally take action.

Change will require making good decisions, establishing important core values in your life, setting priorities, and making commitments. This book will help you identify the values in life that will produce your goals and objectives. High personal character and good habits can be achieved if you want them.

This Series is designed to help you smooth out the path for your life journey. Remember, the key to your success is: "***Decide you want to do it and work at it regularly***."

Free PDF
Living Wisely

The Life Planning Guide

A Quick-Start Guide to Purposeful Living and Wise Decisions!

Discover the five life domains: purpose, people, principles, productivity, and perspective. Wisdom is the ability to apply truth and logic to real-life decisions and produce good outcomes. It influences your choices and will produce action that lasts. Consider and apply the five practical wisdom principles for daily living. (6 pages)

Free PDF: https://getwisdompublishing.com/resource-registration/

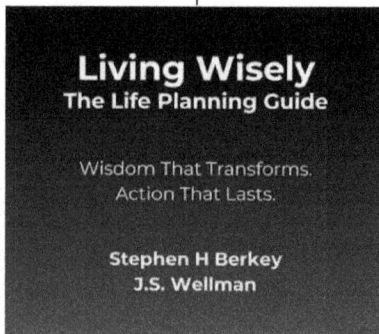

Living Wisely
The Life Planning Guide

Wisdom That Transforms.
Action That Lasts.

Stephen H Berkey
J.S. Wellman

Free PDF

Five Practical Principles For Life

When wisdom meets purpose, transformation follows.

Free PDF
Wise Decision-Making
[Get the ebook version for 99 cents]

You can make good choices.

This free resource provides a project-oriented perspective and gives ten detailed steps to analyze issues/problems to determine a solution. (26 pages)

Good decisions expand your horizons. Don't allow the fear of decision-making paralyze your ability to make good choices. Think through the reasonable alternatives and move forward. When your eyes are on the goal, making good decisions is easier.

Free PDF: https://getwisdompublishing.com/resource-registration/

Kindle ebook for 99 cents: https://www.amazon.com/dp/B09SYGWRVL/

Ebook

Free PDF

Make Thoughtful Decisions!

Good decisions expand your horizons.

INTRODUCTION

Commit to your core values.
They will drive your life!

GENERAL

Core Values are important for everyone! They are valuable for leaders and followers alike. We all need a foundation on which to make decisions. We need to stand on moral principles, demonstrate ethical behavior, or be a role model for others. Core values are necessary to gain respect and maintain your reputation.

Appropriate core values are often the basis for the formation of groups or friendships. They can be the basis for anything from getting hired for a job to getting married. They will often prevent confusion about instructions that might otherwise be misinterpreted. People of high character stand firm on their core values.

Groups and teams need to share similar core values. For example, if an employer places a high value on integrity and honesty, it will be difficult for employees who are careless with the truth to maintain their jobs for any length of time. Employers will often terminate employees who do not adhere to the core values of the organization.

High-performing leaders and teams are looking
for ways to gain competitive advantage.
High performance is often associated with
the existence of core values.

OUR CORE VALUES

This book is about personal core values: that is, values you adopt to support your personal ethical beliefs. Thus, we will discuss the important core values or character traits you might adopt in your life.

To help you better understand what we mean by core values, here are the ten "truths" that Extra-mile Publishing has established as the core values or truths for the Life Planning Series of products:

1. Wise sayings, parables, proverbs, common sense, and street smarts provide an underlying foundation for gaining knowledge, understanding, and wisdom.

2. Honesty, integrity, and living a life based on truth are the foundational character traits for achieving a life of hope, satisfaction, and contentment. This is the first and most important of the five Primary Life Principles:

- be honest, live with integrity, base your life on truth,
- choose your friends wisely,
- choose your words carefully,
- be a diligent and hard worker, and
- make sound financial choices.

3. Life change is possible. You *can* make positive changes and expect good results to follow.

4. All choices have consequences.

5. It is not necessary to change a large number of character traits in order to achieve significant life improvement.

6. The key to making any life change is *intentionality*.

7. Perfection is not possible, but we can achieve significant improvement. Nothing will be attained if you do not try.

8. We will be open about the difficulties, barriers, and walls that one might experience in implementing life change.

9. The ultimate purpose in this series is to develop an effective plan for improving life circumstances. It is not our intent to provide lengthy textbooks on any particular subject.

10. Life is a progressive journey requiring good choices and a solid foundation for the future. Time is needed to implement change. Patience and perseverance will be necessary to achieve the desired results.

Even just a superficial reading of these ten statements will tell you a great deal about the nature and purpose and the Life Planning Series. The core values you choose for yourself will tell a great deal about you, what is important to you, and how you are likely to respond to trials, temptations, and challenges.

WHY READ THIS BOOK

The ideal reader of this book is someone who:

- wants to learn more about the subject of core values,
- is interested in self-improvement or self-growth,
- wants to live a good life with less stress,
- has a history of bad choices or is living in chaos,
- is feeling overwhelmed and is looking for guidance,
- desires to change or improve their life, or
- wants to learn how to make good or better decisions.

Personal growth

We encourage you to make good choices and improve your personal and work life. This process is often referred to as personal growth or personal development. There are many good reasons for pursuing personal growth in your life or business career:

- to find personal peace, meaning, and purpose,
- to gain more control over life circumstances,
- to be more effective in certain skills, abilities or decisions,
- to become more disciplined,
- to expand potential horizons,
- to open new avenues of understanding, or
- to change certain outcomes in your life.

It is our hope that this book will help you identify, focus on, and improve your core values. They will determine the outline of your life.

Employer training

This book can also be used by employers as a guidebook or workbook in providing employee training and development programs for employee growth. Many of these personal core values are similar to the core values of an employer's business. You can use this book to teach and train employees on the nature, value, and importance of both personal and business core values. Each chapter contains a section titled, "Importance to an Employer" that relates the core value to an employer's business.

Note: Employers interested in developing and implementing core values in their business should obtain *Powerful Business Strategies*. See the ad opposite the Table of Contents.

About CHOOSE Core Values

What if one choice could bring clarity and direction to you.? Your life is shaped by the values you choose to live by—whether you realize it or not. *Choose Core Values* helps you take control of those choices, giving you a powerful foundation for making better decisions, improving your relationships, and building a life of meaning and purpose.

This book isn't just about understanding values—it's about discovering *your* values and learning how to apply them in real life. Whether you're feeling stuck, overwhelmed, living in chaos, or simply ready to grow, this guide offers a clear path to lasting change.

You'll discover how to:

- Identify your true core values—and why they matter
- Make better choices by aligning decisions with your values
- Build a life rooted in clarity, character, and direction
- Strengthen your personal integrity and reduce life's stress
- Create a framework for self-growth and meaningful success

Whether you're pursuing personal development, recovering from poor past decisions, or seeking a stronger foundation for life and work, this book will help you build a better future—starting from the inside out.

This book can also be used for coaches, small groups, or workplace development programs, *Choose Core Values* is more than a book—it's a personal growth tool you'll return to again and again.

Take back control of your life—one core value at a time.

THE LIFE PLANNING SERIES

The purpose of this book as well as the Life Planning Series is to encourage you to pursue actions and character traits that will produce a better life. The book series addresses such topics as integrity, choosing friends, guarding your speech, working with diligence, making sound financial decisions, having a positive self- image, leadership, faith, and this book on core values.

This book on core values is different. Rather than one subject there are sixteen – you can see a list of the topics in the Table of Contents.

THE LIFE PLANNING HANDBOOK

This is a unique book in the Life Planning Series. The purpose is to produce a total and complete *Life Plan* for your life. The sections are:

1. Life Principles and Character Attributes
2. Habits
3. Friends and Family Relationships
4. Work and Work Ethic
5. Education
6. Community Service
7. Money and Wealth
8. Health
9. Spiritual

The planning process in the Handbook will examine your skills and abilities, your personal life values, priorities, and commitments. The book will help you identify your life goals and create action steps to achieve those goals. It also includes additional help in the Appendix.

These books will generate purpose,
direction, and growth in your life.

CONSEQUENCES

People are constantly making choices about both significant and insignificant issues. Choices shape the course of our lives. They are inevitable and can produce either good or bad results. Some people learn a great deal from the consequences of their actions while others seem oblivious and never learn anything.

By definition, consequences occur as a result of something else happening. They are the outcome of some other action. However, they do not always occur immediately. They could take a while, even years. This is often one of the reasons that we make poor choices – the consequences do not occur immediately and because of this we think there will never be consequences.

Physical consequences are a law of nature. If you touch a hot stove you will get burned. If you walk in front of a speeding truck you will be injured. Behaviors, too, have predictable consequences. If you cheat and lie your reputation will be damaged. If you are not dependable and reliable, people will not trust you.

The actual consequences you experience will vary depending on your circumstances, but there will be consequences nonetheless. The degree of the consequence will also vary, but do not be fooled into thinking small actions are insignificant. Even small actions can produce significant consequences.

We reap what we sow

In a number of his proverbs, King Solomon suggests that doing what is right is to be preferred over wickedness. King Solomon was known world-wide for his great wisdom. He wrote and recorded many proverbs recognized for their practical insight and wisdom. He describes the nature of righteousness as being immovable and that it will stand above the wicked.

Is your desire for doing what is "right" rooted deeply or is it planted in shallow soil that can easily be washed away? Solomon indicated that the wicked would ultimately be overthrown and that the righteous would survive because their character had roots that were deep and impossible to dislodge.

Solomon argued that it is better to be on the side of the righteous. The reasoning is the same as the man who builds his house, business, or life on rock versus sand. If we build on sand (questionable ways) then our hopes and plans will never stand up against the storms of life. If we build on rock (high character) our plans will hold firm.

We do reap what we sow and if we sow badly because we have rejected what is right, the wise counsel of friends, or our core values, we will reap the negative consequences. Those who think they know everything frequently reject wisdom and follow their own plans and schemes. It has been said that those who insist on following their own ways will often end up choking on them.

Choices produce consequences
which direct the course of life.
Consequences shape lives.
Therefore, count the cost!

BARRIERS

Difficulties and barriers can be overcome if you are determined to find a solution. It's a lot easier to make changes in life if you are receiving guidance and help. In addition to our books we suggest finding someone to join you in improving your core values. If you cannot find someone to participate with you, find someone you can meet with weekly or periodically to discuss your progress, your difficulties, your needs, and most of all, your successes.

Here are some effective ways to overcome personal barriers:

1. Recognize that many barriers are in reality just excuses.
2. Recruit a support person (friend) to hold you accountable.
3. Recruit others to do it with you. Push each other.
4. Recruit support from your family.
5. If time is a hurdle – work it out. Adjust your priorities.

But, don't expect change, improvement, or miracles overnight.

"Being challenged in life is inevitable,
being defeated is optional."
Roger Crawford

Chapter 1
Integrity

INTEGRITY LIFE PRINCIPLE:
Be honest, live with integrity, and base your life on truth.

"One word of truth
outweighs the whole world."
Alexander Solzhenitsyn

NOTE:
This chapter is *generally* a summary or paraphrase of the book *Choose Integrity* in our Life Planning Series. It is included in this book because it is the <u>foundational core value</u> and as such it needs to be readily available to readers of this book. However, if honesty and integrity and particularly truth are important to you, we would recommend that you acquire a copy of *Choose Integrity*, which goes into more depth on this subject

GENERAL

Of all the personal characteristics, we believe integrity to be the basic core value. Of the sixteen core values discussed in this book, the most fundamental is being a person of honesty and integrity. If you adhere to this core value, it is much easier to achieve success and live a good life. Honesty, integrity, and truth are the gateways to being the best person you can be. You will never be able to be all you can be if these three traits are not an inherent part of your life.

Any contractor or builder will tell you that the most important part of a house is the foundation. A foundation that is not level and placed on solid ground will create problems in every phase of the building process. If floors are not level and walls not plumb, the construction ultimately may need to be torn down. Honesty and integrity should be the foundational core values of your life.

If you live with integrity, you will inherently possess a number of other good character traits. Integrity will produce a life in which you are dependable, reliable, upright, and a person of good reputation. If you are truthful you will be sincere, incorruptible, and just. You will be guided by and make choices based on truth. You will not cheat to gain advantage. You will not be devious, deceptive, crafty, scheming, double-dealing, false, or deceptive. This is why honesty, integrity, and truth are the cornerstones for a better life. It is why many successful businesses include some version of these traits in their core values.

Our personal character is the foundation of who we are. It determines what we say and what we do as well as the habits we form. Our character reflects what we really believe and what we value. If we have the inherent desire to do what is right we will have a high regard for truth and integrity.

**Make it your primary life goal to be honest,
to live with integrity, and to base your life on truth!**

HONESTY

Honesty means that you speak the truth. You do not lie. It also means that you do not cheat. You would not defraud, deceive, or misinform someone, whether it is a friend, an acquaintance, or even a stranger.

This concept can be illustrated by the color white. If something is true and honest, then it is pure white. If there is any gray then it is no longer white. It may be referred to as dirty white or off-white. Truth and honesty are like that. They are pure. There is no such thing as partial truth. Something is either true or is not true.

You are either honest or you're not. If there is any gray mixed into your honesty, then it is no longer honesty. Little white lies should be called little gray lies. Partial truth and partial honesty do not exist.

Honesty in all things

If you are honest, then you will be honest in both the big and small things of life. It doesn't matter if it is stealing pencils from your employer or stealing a car. The honest person does neither. There is no such thing as a little lie, a little deception, or a little cheating. If we cheat at little things we most likely will cheat at big things. And the easier it is for us to steal little things the more likely it is that we will consider stealing things of significant value.

If you know someone who does not cheat on the little things, that person is not likely to cheat on big things. You can trust a person who demonstrates honesty and dependability in the little things of life or a career. An honest man is honest with pennies as well as with millions.

Stealing

What's the difference between stealing a $5 product from the mall or one that costs $5000? Technically nothing: both are stealing. Certainly one is a more significant loss to the owner. If you believe it is acceptable to steal small items without deserving any punishment, then you will also find it acceptable to lie about small things.

The problem occurs when someone must decide what is small and what is large. Who has such authority? How much authority is required to define what is important and what is not? What if one small thievery combined with a hundred other small thieveries was enough to put someone out of business?

Lies, big and small

A big danger in little lies is that they can lead to the habit of lying. Instead of just lying about trivia or matters of little consequence, we begin lying to protect ourselves from our own poor choices. If we do not want to look bad to our friends or if we fail to complete a promise, it becomes easy to lie. Lying can become a very convenient part of our lifestyle, allowing us to make excuses for simply not being reliable.

"If a person doesn't lie,
he won't have that much to remember!"
Abe Lincoln

Society acceptance

Society changes when dishonesty is rampant throughout the general public. Cheating or any dishonest behavior can become a way of life and be accepted as a normal state of affairs. For example, you can't do business in some countries and even with some city or state governments without paying bribes. Dishonesty left unchecked becomes a cancer controlling how business is conducted.

It can become so bad that dishonesty becomes the norm. When the general public decides everyone is doing it, they believe they also must cheat in order to survive. This is what happened in the sport of professional bicycle racing between 1990 and 2010. You may have read about the drug scandals involving Lance Armstrong. But Armstrong was not the only one cheating. The sport was overrun by cheating and drug abuse.

Then, of course, the cover-up begins. Everyone lies about the true environment, hoping not to be caught. The sad thing is that the lying just builds up until it explodes. The liars begin thinking that what they are doing is acceptable behavior. They believe their own lies. They may even have a very high opinion of themselves while they are living a lie. But eventually the lie is exposed and the inevitable cover-up begins, leading to the undeniable truth. Then the lies evaporate and the liar is exposed! *Lies make life miserable!*

Liars

Liars are usually caught or found out. Fortunes can be lost and reputations destroyed. Liars can lose their families and friends. How does this happen? Difficulties tend to haunt those who live off lies. Marriages are destroyed by lies and cheating. The overall result is that the liar ultimately gets caught and their dishonesty will cause various levels of difficulty, suffering, and even time in prison. Some have even committed suicide because they could not live with the shame of public disclosure.

Immediate admission of error or misdoing is the best solution to righting a wrong. If Lance Armstrong had admitted his cheating early on and offered to help fix the problem, his life would have been much different and his standing in the eyes of society would be much higher today. He might even be considered a person of high character, even though he was initially caught in a web of lies.

> *"I have met men who are habitual liars.*
> *They have lied so long that they no longer can distinguish*
> *between the truth and a lie. Their sensitivity to sin*
> *has been almost completely deadened."*
> Billy Graham

Honesty does matter

Being honest is like eating a sweet piece of chocolate. Why? Because it is so desirable and sweet it can produce a very comfortable and satisfying feeling. Honesty should be desired like foods that give us great pleasure. Knowing you are honest and your life is based on truth will produce a life of satisfaction and far less stress than one that exists on lies.

Do you know anyone you consider a liar? Are they one of your friends or associates? Do you hang out with them? People who are habitual liars are very difficult to live or work with. They produce great stress in your life. A trustworthy friend can be appreciated and trusted. A life of honesty is one that others will admire. A trustworthy person is one whom you want as a friend or business associate.

Dishonesty

How do you react when you catch someone lying to you? Are you disappointed in their unreliability? Do you react in a way that would condone their lying and dishonesty? Do you respond in a way that allows them to think you have no personal standards with respect to the truth? If you imply you understand or condone lying, you have not done yourself or the liar any favors.

The liar will probably perceive that you have little concern for truth, thus, you are not one who can be trusted. This could have significant impact on your reputation with the liar and anyone he tells about your behavior. The liar will continue to lie to you and about you, creating all kinds of grief in your life.

Confronting dishonesty and unreliability can be difficult. It can be stressful. But allowing it to continue will not make a bad situation better; it will only get worse. You must make it clear to the liar that you know the truth, that you are disappointed in the behavior, and that you hope it never happens again.

"A liar deceives himself more than anyone,
for he believes he can remain a person
of good character when he cannot."
Richelle E. Goodrich

INTEGRITY

Integrity is the practice of being honest trustworthy, and true to a set of moral standards. It might be suggested that integrity is conformity to doing the right thing, even when no one is watching. Someone who lives by integrity will be virtuous, honorable, and upright. They will have a commitment to ethical and moral behavior. Integrity produces actions that are esteemed by others. Our actions, not our words, demonstrate whether we have integrity.

Integrity is a shield

Honesty and truth will shield you from deceit, gossip, slander, and many other forms of evil. Integrity allows you to have a sense of calm and security, living without fear of lies being exposed and disrupting or even destroying your life. Those who are dishonest will become known and typically have few friends or associates. Life for the dishonest person is often not very pleasant. Integrity will protect you from the consequences of a life built on dishonesty.

People respect integrity

Hearing a good report about the character of someone of high integrity can be like money in the bank for the one being praised. People with integrity never need to talk about their own character because others will do it for them. Integrity leads to satisfaction and contentment. You cannot be content if your time is in chaos because of dishonesty or deceit. When your life is spent avoiding people to whom you have lied, formulating new lies, or getting others to lie to protect you, life is not comfortable or very peaceful.

Integrity will draw people to your side or to your cause. You will find assistance much easier to find when you live with integrity compared to the person that is untrustworthy. Why would people waste their time with someone who is dishonest, casual with the truth, or who cares little for doing what is right?

> *"Your image is what people think of you*
> *and your integrity is who you really are."*
> John Maxwell

Stress

Being dishonest creates various problems that produce stress and often a great deal of anxiety:

- A liar lives in mountains of lies, distrust, guilt, and even fear.
- A liar's relationships with others will be difficult to maintain.
- A liar will often be burdened with shame.
- A bad reputation can cause serious problems for one trying to provide for a family.
- A liar will not be considered for job opportunities because of his unreliability

> *"Perhaps the surest test of an individual's*
> *integrity is his refusal to do or say anything*
> *that would damage his self-respect."*
> Thomas S. Monson

COMPROMISE

The art of compromise is often the key to reaching agreements with others. This is a frequent process in business for obtaining the best arrangement for all parties involved. The ability to compromise in this manner is considered a proper and appropriate means to produce working relationships that both parties can endorse.

On the other hand, if I compromise my values or my word I will normally be looked on with scorn and distrust by my friends and associates. Or, if I won't compromise on very unimportant issues then I may be considered hardheaded and stubborn because of my refusal to agree to what is considered a reasonable compromise.

Can you compromise and still be trustworthy? Certainly! Compromise does not necessarily mean that one fails to keep a promise or is unreliable. This term is more often used in business but it can apply to relationship as well. If I compromise my personal core values, I may only be cheating myself. If I cheat or lie I am impacting relationships between friends, family, or business associates, and this is where being trustworthy becomes a serious concern or valuable commodity.

If you stand for the truth, claim to be loyal, swear to be trustworthy, but compromise your promises or standards, then compromise is bad and can produce severe consequences. A wise saying suggests, "When you have to compromise yourself or your ethical standards for the people around you, it's time to change the people around you."

However, in settling disputes or negotiating contracts, compromise can be positive. In such situations the parties are making mutual concessions or accommodations in order to arrive at a mutually agreeable result. In such circumstances people make concessions in order to receive the benefit of a contractual agreement.

Dale Carnegie said in his book, *How to Win Friends and Influence People*, "The highest levels of influence are reached when generosity and trustworthiness surround your behavior." Think about this statement as it relates to compromise. If you trusted someone and they were generous, meaning they were willing to give away something that was of valuable to them, would you also be willing to be generous and give up something of value? That is what typically happens in contractual compromise.

Compromising with people of high character usually produces a win-win situation for both parties.

"Learn the wisdom of compromise,
for it is better to bend a little than to break."
(Anonymous)

Compromise when life is difficult

Difficulties should not impact your commitment to the truth. Just because life gets difficult is not a good reason for compromising your personal values or business standards. If you cannot deliver on a promise, tell the truth. Nothing is gained by lying. You may gain some time, but the lie will be found out. Dennis Prager has said, "Compromise, while at times morally necessary or at least justifiable, is more often only the first permission for a person (or society) to begin a long downhill descent." In other words, compromise is sometimes needed but it can be a slippery slope and we must be very sure about the choices we are making.

People whose word cannot be trusted will find life difficult. Trying to be the best you can be while being untrustworthy is not really possible.

> *"All compromise is based on give and take,*
> *but there can be no give and take on fundamentals.*
> *Any compromise on mere fundamentals is surrender.*
> *For it is all give and no take."*
> Mahatma Gandhi

Standing firm

Expect opposition or push-back from people who do not hold your same values. This is often verbal and may be accompanied by threats to cancel a relationship. Dropping certain relationships or leaving a group may be the best course of action for you. Don't waste time with people or activities that oppose your core values.

Standing firm means that you ignore the peer pressure of friends or associates when the suggested action would violate your core values. One of the best ways to hold fast to your values is to have friends and advisors who support you in trying circumstances. If the situation involves an employer-employee relationship, your employer will certainly support your adherence to their company core values. But if it's personal, the stress and anxiety can be difficult. This is the time when it's crucial to have good friends that can support and advise you.

Alternatively, if we won't compromise on less important matters we are often considered stubborn or obstinate. It is important to understand your circumstances and know what is important in both personal and business situations. For example, you could choose to extend credit to an old customer who is experiencing a temporary downturn in their business, even though granting such extension is not consistent with your rules and guidelines. Logic and good sense should dictate when to adhere to your rules or principles and when to make a reasonable compromise.

Five practical tips

1. Know who shares your values. Stand firm with others who have similar core values.
2. Be humble. Do not consider yourself better than others. A superior attitude is never a good idea.
3. Be selfless, thankful, and generous to others – even those who do not share your values.
4. Be gracious and look out for the needs of others.
5. Hold onto your core values and make others aware of your standards.

> *"If you have integrity nothing else matters.*
> *If you don't have integrity nothing else matters."*
> Alan K. Simpson

TRUTH

Does truth really matter? Yes, dishonesty will cause most people a great deal of distress. This occurs because one becomes ashamed or feels guilty about their behavior. Guilt is a big factor in living with dishonesty. There is also the ongoing stress of keeping lies alive and the worry of being found out. Liars have great difficulty in maintaining relationships, and lying on the job is an excellent way to find yourself looking for a new career.

Truth is fundamental to having high character. It cannot be achieved without a commitment to honesty. The person who gains a reputation for being a liar will find that reputation very difficult to overcome.

It is also dangerous to shade the truth. If you claim something is true, but it is only 90% true, then it's not true. This is a concept that many people struggle with. It does not become true just because someone declares it to be true. Absolute truth does exist. Something does not become untrue simply because someone chooses not to believe it or because they claim it to be untrue.

Value truth

Friends and business associates appreciate honest people. They value others who speak the truth and act in truth. Leaders in particular value honesty. Leaders cannot lead alone. They must trust in the loyalty and veracity of followers to deliver both accurate and truthful information. Even dictators must depend on the honesty and loyalty of some other people – often their personal guards.

Truth is everlasting, but lies last only until they are found out. What does it mean that truth endures and lies do not? Falsehoods and lies are generally found out eventually, producing hurt, trouble, and often conflict. But truth will last because it does not change. Time does not change truth. What is true today is true tomorrow. Lies must be replaced by more lies to sustain their delusion.

History is like truth. The facts are that Columbus sailed to America and slaves were imported from Africa, no matter how distasteful those facts may be. The holocaust did happen and no amount of unbelief will change the facts. Mistakes in the past should teach us lessons, not be altered or covered up.

Truth can be dangerous

Can truth really be dangerous? This statement was probably not true a hundred years ago, but life has changed dramatically in the last fifty years. For example, today you may be held accountable for the truth and have to publically demonstrate that something is true.

You can be shamed, rejected, or ignored for your position supporting the truth. All the logical arguments in the world may not change the minds of certain opponents. In today's society we find people who attack the speaker personally in an attempt to discredit the truth.

Some believe that if you proclaim lies long enough and loud enough people will begin to believe the lies are truth. Sad!

Depending on the nature of the situation you might be tempted to shade the truth rather than face the consequences of the truth. Thus, lies become accepted as truth because the problem of discrediting the lies is either dangerous, time consuming, or expensive. It simply becomes easier to ignore the lie. This often produces apathy on the part of those who know the truth. If you are one who prefers to avoid conflict and not to confront lies, you may find a commitment to honesty and integrity very difficult at times.

If you compromise the truth, you are likely to compromise other related character traits. If you are afraid of what others think it will be challenging for you to tell the truth, because there will always be people who disagree with you because they do not like the truth.

Your words are extremely important in this age when truth is often marginalized in favor of political, business, and personal agendas. Therefore, even when you tell the truth, if it conflicts with someone else's agenda, you can find yourself ridiculed or attacked. You may also be forced to defend the truth. People today often think they can do and say anything in order to achieve their own agendas.

Therefore, it is important that you are both truthful and careful how you tell that truth. You must choose your words carefully.

> ***Truth and its implications today are not***
> ***what they were only several generations ago.***
> ***Choose your words carefully!***

Reasons to tell the truth

Truth allows you to avoid making decisions based on erroneous thoughts or opinions. It helps establish valid understanding and opinions. Speaking truth gives you peace and satisfaction that you have not misled others or yourself.

Truth demonstrates to others that you care. It supports your reputation while assisting you in building meaningful relationships.

One of the most important characteristics of truth is that it creates trust. Effective communication is impossible without honesty.

Lies generally accomplish no good purpose and will often make a bad situation worse. Lies can mask a more serious situation that should be addressed. Such lies seldom remain a secret. The truth will become known and the liar is left to explain himself, or slink away red-faced.

Honesty produces contentment and satisfaction.
There is no contentment in dishonesty,
bad behavior, deceit, or evil.
We must speak the truth and then act it out.

LEADERS

Leaders must know the truth, speak the truth, and reward the truth. The absolute rule is "Be truthful." Lies about people, products, or capabilities have destroyed many leaders and organizations.

Integrity and honesty are core values that leaders _must_ possess. An organization of any size will not be competitive and may not survive unless employees are honest. Leaders who do not display these qualities cannot be trusted to lead an organization. Ultimately they will fail and probably do great damage to the organization.

No matter the circumstances, core values of an organization are not to be violated. In well-run companies, anyone found violating the core values of the organization will be fired immediately. Good leaders demand that core values be followed in their organizations.

Ethical leadership comes down to each individual deciding if he or she is willing to uphold their core values, regardless of whether or not a specific Code of Conduct exists. Good leaders build their careers on a set of core values regardless of whether their organization has a formal Code of Conduct. Those values vary between individuals but will normally include most of the characteristics discussed in this book.

In general, honesty, respect, and trust are the centerpieces of a Code of Conduct. Valued leaders are always accountable for their words and actions. When a good leader makes a mistake, he should be the first to admit it. The focus then becomes on correctly identifying the error and finding effective solutions, not on blame or censure. A leader who wants honesty and integrity from his team must exhibit those same characteristics himself.

> *"Leadership can be defined by one word: 'honesty'.*
> *You must be honest with the players and*
> *honest with yourself."*
> Earl Weaver

PRACTICAL TIPS

1. Be cautious what you say on social media.
2. Communicate promises clearly.
3. Don't make promises you can't keep.
4. Associate with other people of integrity.
5. Establish integrity-related core values.
6. Put truth and integrity above self-esteem. Be humble.
7. Be accountable for what you do. Admit mistakes.
8. Give grace to others when they struggle with trust.
9. Listen and learn from mistakes or correction.
10. Be open and willing to change.
11. Overcome pride if it impacts your ability to live with integrity.
12. Do not cheat on anything, big or small.

IMPORTANCE TO AN EMPLOYER

Integrity is an essential characteristic that fosters trust, promotes ethical behavior, and contributes to a positive work environment. An employee with integrity brings numerous benefits to an organization and creates a foundation for long-term success.

First and foremost, integrity builds trust. Trust is vital for smooth operations and successful business relationships. An employee with integrity consistently acts honestly, ensuring that their actions align with their words. This consistency builds trust among colleagues, superiors, and clients.

Employees who uphold high ethical standards act in accordance with both legal and moral principles and are more likely to make ethical decisions and adhere to the organization's policies and codes of conduct. This commitment to ethical behavior reduces the risk of misconduct and safeguards the organization's reputation.

Employees with integrity serve as role models for their peers. Their consistent display of honesty and ethical behavior will influence the workplace environment and encourage others to follow suit. They contribute to a culture of integrity in which ethical conduct is valued.

Integrity-driven employees tend to be highly reliable as well as accountable because they take ownership of their responsibilities and deliver on their commitments. Employers can depend on them to act responsibly and fulfill their work obligations.

Clients, partners, and customers appreciate working with individuals and organizations they can trust. An employee who exemplifies integrity enhances the organization's reputation and credibility in the eyes of others. This can lead to stronger client relationships and increased customer loyalty.

Finally, employees with integrity demonstrate strong character and moral values which normally align with the organization's mission and values. Their actions reflect positively on the organization and contribute to its overall brand identity. Employers recognize the importance of having employees who embody theses values because they serve as ambassadors for its culture and reputation.[0]

CONCLUSION

Some believe life is a contest and they must use any and all means to win the game. Therefore being devious or deceptive is acceptable behavior because the goal is to come out on top. These people are often very competitive and they may not be concerned how they win, as long as they win. Their attitude is to win at all costs. They may not even think of their activities as competition, but simply the normal game of life, business, or politics.

But what happens between you and your "opponent" if you win some contest, negotiation, or business client because you were deceptive or under-handed? You will lose trust: the only unknown is when! Your opponent will never want to deal with you again. Once your attitudes and shady actions are made known, your reputation can be destroyed.

Deceptive people are usually disliked. Their overly-competitive nature makes them undesirable friends or associates.

You may wonder why you shouldn't use everything at your disposal to beat business rivals, sports opponents, or those you are competing with for the next career promotion or business deal. Isn't being smart a virtue? Yes, but being devious or cunning is not a virtue except in the eyes of other schemers. Being smart is a virtue if it is used in a good way and not to gain *unfair* advantage. If you are confused or unsure of what to do, ask yourself, "How would I feel if what I am about to do would be done to me?"

> *"There is no better test of a man's integrity*
> *than his behavior when he is wrong."*
> Marvin Williams

Honesty and integrity provide an atmosphere that draws others to you. They will encourage effective groups to form around you because people trust the standards and environment you represent.

A truthful environment encourages others to offer their perspective on questions, projects, ideas, and even relationships. When opposing views are discouraged, truth will often be masked in platitudes and flattery. There are generally no serious consequences for being open and truthful. Individuals will be open and true when they experience others who display openness with integrity. There is no reason to be closed and protective if a group honors those who tell the truth.

Honesty is the foundation for true relationships. Integrity is an invitation for others to join your circle of associates. People with similar core values support each other in both times of stress and success. If you are true, sincere, and genuine, you will attract others who are trustworthy. Truth is a magnet for people seeking friends, co-workers, employers, or customers they can trust.

> *Think before you speak and act.*
> *Your reputation is important!*

EXAMPLES: Integrity Core Value Statements

1. I value honesty and always strive to speak the truth, even when it is difficult.

2. I believe in acting with transparency and ensuring my actions align with my words.

3. I am committed to upholding high ethical standards in all aspects of my life.

4. I prioritize treating others with fairness, respect, and dignity.

5. I value trustworthiness and strive to earn and maintain the trust of others.

6. I believe in doing what is morally right, even when faced with challenges or temptations.

7. I am committed to delivering on my promises and following through on my commitments.

8. I value personal accountability and hold myself to the same standards I expect from others.

9. I prioritize consistency in my behavior and decision-making, guided by my moral compass.

10. I value integrity in all my interactions, whether personal or professional.

MY PERSONAL CORE VALUE – Integrity

Adopt or confirm your core value. If integrity is already a core value, or if you want to establish it as a core value, write your personal statement in the space below. You may want to use the examples above as guides to draft your Personal Core Value Statement. Make it short, succinct, and meaningful to you. Something you can easily remember.

Integrity Core Value:

_____

_____

_____

_____

_____

_____

_____

DISCUSSION AND THOUGHT QUESTIONS

1. There is an anonymous saying about compromise: "Many things are worse than defeat, and compromise with evil is one of them." Do you agree with this? Why? Why not?

2. What reasons would you list for the importance of integrity?

3. How is integrity demonstrated in family, friendships, or work groups?

4. Do you believe there are times when it is appropriate to lie?

5. In the list of "Practical Tips" which one would work best for you? Why? Which one would be the most difficult for you?

6. What does integrity mean to you personally, and how important is it to you?

7. Can you recall a time when someone's lack of integrity affected you or others around you? How did it impact the situation and your perception of that person?

8. How does integrity impact your reputation and how others perceive who you are?

9. What are the potential consequences if you compromise your integrity for short-term gains?

10. How can integrity be maintained in situations where personal interests might conflict with ethical principles?

11. Can you think of professions or industries in which integrity is particularly crucial? Why is it important in those contexts?

12. How does acting with integrity enhance your self-esteem and belief in your abilities?

NOTES

I want to do the following:

a. _____
b. _____
c. _____
d. _____

I want to remember:

a. _____
b. _____
c. _____
d. _____

Action Challenge: Reflect on a recent situation where your integrity was tested. How did you respond? What could you have done differently to more closely align with your values, and what specific steps can you take now to reinforce your commitment to integrity in future situations?

Chapter 2
Trustworthiness

TRUSTWORTHINESS LIFE PRINCIPLE:
I will be dependable and reliable.

*"The highest levels of influence are reached
when generosity and trustworthiness
surround your behavior."*
Unknown

GENERAL

One of the fundamental aspects of a trustworthy person is the ability to keep a secret. Being trustworthy and being honest are very close cousins. You cannot be trustworthy and be dishonest. Being trustworthy means others can rely on your words and your promises. If you are trustworthy you carry through on what you said or promised and your friends and associates have total confidence in you.

Merriam-Webster defines being trustworthy as belief that someone is reliable, honest, or effective. If you are trustworthy, others can rely on your ability to do something. You will not commit to doing things you cannot do. Others will have high confidence that you are reliable and dependable. You can be trusted, not just when it is easy, but in times of crisis. Thus, you are deserving of respect. You are sincere, genuine, and worthy of the confidence of others.

If you were to ask a friend what it means to be trustworthy, you might receive some of the following responses:

- I will always stand firm on my word.
- I will have the courage to confront authority if necessary to fulfill a promise.
- I will never break my word or promise even if I incur some difficulty or hardship.
- I will not be intimidated by the threat of push-back.
- I will always stand firm in my beliefs and core values.

- I will always be more concerned about disappointing a friend than gaining an advantage.
- I will be totally loyal and work constantly to maintain trust.
- I will not allow personal difficulties impact my commitment to keeping my promises.

What would it mean in your life to have complete trust in someone? What would they have to say or do? Typically a reputation for being trustworthy is not created because someone keeps their promise on just a few occasions. Becoming trustworthy is like a good reputation: it is gained by consistent performance over time. You develop true confidence in someone when your relationship has been refined by trustworthy performance, sometimes in difficult circumstances.

If it costs nothing to be trustworthy then what is the evidence that one can actually be trusted? If I promise to show up at some location when I am already going to be in the neighborhood, it is not proof I am trustworthy. But if I show up in the middle of the night when you have an emergency: that means something!

BEING TRUSTWORTHY

Enemies will find it difficult to find weaknesses to exploit in people who are not negligent or corrupt. If you are honest and trustworthy it will be difficult to damage your reputation. There will be no basis to threaten you if you have done nothing wrong.

Friends want people in their lives they can trust. Employers want people with high character representing them. Constituents want people of high character in government fighting for them. Thus, trustworthy men and women are in high demand.

Being trustworthy is often more than being honest and keeping promises – it can mean being present, being available in emergencies, or going the extra mile. You cannot be underhanded if you are trustworthy. Being untrustworthy may imply you are a person who lies, cheats, takes bribes, or may mean you are not a good person. If you are trustworthy you may have some faults, but your reputation is of high repute. Your word can be trusted

Many claim to be trustworthy but they are sometimes fickle and unfaithful. It can be difficult to find a true trustworthy friend or employee! This is a sad commentary on the state of the human condition. Many of us are only "partially" trustworthy. We may loudly proclaim our dedication, but the reality is that we have no intention of fulfilling the boasts we make. We find it easier to fulfill our promises when there is something in it for us.

The challenge in identifying trustworthy people is that you have to witness such character in order to know that someone can actually be trusted. There is no way to interview a candidate for a job and determine if they are untrustworthy, unless they unwittingly admit it. Thus, employers will be cautious about who they trust until that employee demonstrates they are true to their word.

If you are going to associate with or work closely with someone, you want them to have the same kind of core values that you possess. If your values are not similar there will eventually be serious conflict. You want associates, co-workers, and friends who have high personal character and can be trusted.

> *"Trust is like a vase, once it's broken, though you*
> *can fix it, the vase will never be same again."*
> Walter Anderson

Be reliable

An unreliable person cannot be trusted. Untrustworthy people are like a sore tooth that is not cared for. It will get worse! It is difficult to associate with people who break promises, or simply don't follow through with the commitments they have made. When instructions are ignored or promises are broken, it is extremely hard to maintain a relationship of any kind. Like rotten teeth the relationship will keep getting worse until the problem is fixed. The decay must be eradicated because it will spread. Being unreliable is almost a perfect synonym for being untrustworthy.

> *"Trust is always earned, never given."*
> R. Williams

Be dependable

Being dependable is also an important aspect of being trustworthy. For example, if someone is sick or injured can you be depended on to give the doctor an accurate report? Can you be depended on to go and bring back help? Can you be depended on to provide reasonable assistance? What can you be depended on to do or not do?

Most of us are not involved with doctors so our words and actions are typically not a matter of life and death. A more probable scenario might be whether you are honest and sincere with your friends or bosses and will you deliver on your promises? Can you provide a clear and frank assessment of the abilities, strengths, and weaknesses of an associate or friend? Can you provide an accurate assessment of the status of a project? Or will you be influenced by other forces and provide inaccurate information, meaning you are not dependable.

If you cannot provide a trustworthy assessment of a person, project, or situation, you are likely to be considered undependable. If you are the one who receives faulty information, you are going to be very disappointed in the source of the information. If you are the one not delivering a dependable report to someone, it could ultimately mean the loss of a friendship, demotion, or even loss of a job.

Being trustworthy or dependable also means you keep a confidence and can be relied on to deliver confidential information. You do not reveal information that should be kept confidential. This could be embarrassing information about a friend or important information concerning the inner workings of your employer. Dependable people not only gain reputations for being trustworthy but the people they associate with or represent also gain respect.

No one wants to do business with people or companies that have a reputation for not keeping promises or falling short on what they promised to deliver. Friends, associates, and customers are lost daily because someone did not deliver on a promise.

Do you have friends or associates who are undependable? What would you trust them with? They may not intentionally lie or fabricate false stories, but they simply cannot be trusted to deliver the promised or expected result. Make sure you do not acquire a reputation for being undependable because you will never be given anything important to do. People know you cannot be trusted to perform or deliver as expected.

"Put more trust in nobility of character
than in an oath."
Solon

Be loyal

Being trustworthy creates loyalty in friends and followers. If you are loyal it means that you give complete and constant support to a person or a group. It means you have unswerving allegiance, are faithful, and steadfast. If you are loyal you will remain in the good graces of friends and associates, even if you stumble or make mistakes along the way.

It is important to accurately evaluate the character of the people you associate with, whether in business or your personal life. There are many who claim to be loyal but when the time comes to demonstrate that loyalty they are nowhere to be found. They simply do not deliver!

A leader must inspire loyalty. Loyalty is created by high character, including being trustworthy. No one intentionally follows dishonest or uncaring leaders unless they themselves share the same negative qualities. Leaders without a following are just talking to themselves because no one is really listening.

Truth and integrity create loyalty. Being honest in all you say and do will ultimately win the day, even though the truth might hurt a bit.

"Loyalty isn't grey. It's black and white.
You're either loyal completely, or not loyal at all."
Sharnay

TRUSTWORTHY FRIENDS!

When you are in a position of trust, someone is depending on you. It may be as simple as helping a needy neighbor. It may be trusting that you will not take unfair advantage of someone in a difficult position. It may be doing what is right, perhaps more than what is legally or contractually required. Good friends, associates, and businesses watch out and care for those they can trust. There is little to be gained by risking your reputation for someone you cannot trust.

There is a proverb that says, "*The wounds of a friend are trustworthy, but the kisses of an enemy are excessive*" (Proverbs 27:6). The "wounds" can refer to, correction, or even discipline. If such wound comes from a friend or close associate, it is intended to protect, fix, or improve some situation. It is wise to take seriously correction from a friend or trusted associate. Why? A friend can be trusted. Do you want correction from a friend or an enemy? I'll take a friend because they have my best interests at heart, even when the correction may be difficult to hear.

Those who do not have your true interest in mind may shower you with flattery, lies, or promises of gain. If it sounds too good to be true, it probably is! It is good to remember who your friends are and who are just acquaintances or associates. They will have different objectives and agendas.

Keep your eyes on the important people in your life. If you have friends who demonstrate honesty and trust, protect them. Copy their ways! Do what they do! Imitate the ways of those who have outstanding reputations. Observe what they do and learn from them.

> **"If you succeed in cheating someone, don't think that the person is a fool. Realize that the person trusted you much, more than you deserve."**
> Unknown

CONSEQUENCES

There are consequences for being disloyal, undependable, or unreliable. The consequences will generally be related to the nature of the offense. It can be the loss of friendship, loss of a customer, loss of advancement, loss of face, loss of intimacy, etc. For example, a swindler may become poor. An extrovert who is overly social may find that he or she is shunned and becomes lonely. A person with responsibility or authority may lose their position of power.

If you cannot be trusted you <u>will</u> suffer. The nature, timing, and degree of loss will vary with the significance of the situation. Those who cannot be trusted are often under constant tension because their offenses could blow up in their face at any time. You do not want to be in the vicinity when the explosion occurs.

FINAL ADVICE

Trustworthy friends and associates may be scarce. Take the time and energy necessary to find intelligent and energetic people whom you can trust. Their advice will be invaluable. You can build strong relationships with people who are trustworthy. If you make friends with people who have poor reputations you will lose respect and your own reputation may be negatively impacted because of their questionable character. On the other hand, you will be admired by others if your friends are people of high character.

Adopt core values that are important in your life. Respect is a common characteristic for those that are trustworthy. Honesty and integrity are the foundational character traits for living a life of high character. You cannot be untrustworthy and expect to live a stress-free life.

Being trustworthy in a world that is increasingly complex and demanding can be challenging. There will be many opportunities in life to stretch the truth, overstate what you can deliver, or exaggerate reality. Make the following your personal motto:

- I am believable, I am reliable, and I keep my promises.
- I am dependable. I keep my word and commitments.
- I am honest. I don't lie. I have high integrity.
- I keep secrets. I do not share what is confidential.
- I am loyal. I am steadfast. I am faithful.
- I am sincere, genuine, and authentic.
- I am trustworthy!

> *"Trust is the assured reliance on another's integrity."*
> David Richo

PRACTICAL TIPS

Here are some easy-to-implement tips for demonstrating or practicing the personal core value of being trustworthy:

1. Keep your promises. Follow through on commitments you make, whether they are big or small.

2. Be honest. Speak the truth and avoid exaggerations or deceit.

3. Maintain confidentiality. Respect the privacy of others and keep sensitive information confidential. Don't gossip.

4. Admit mistakes. Take responsibility for your actions and quickly admit when you make a mistake.

5. Be reliable. Show up on time and complete tasks within the agreed-upon timeframe.

6. Be consistent. Act in a manner that aligns with your values consistently over time.

7. Be loyal. Support and stand up for the people you care about, especially when they're not present.

8. Boundaries. Honor personal boundaries and avoid pressuring others to disclose more than they're comfortable with.

9. Be accountable. Take ownership of your actions and accept the consequences of your decisions.

10. Demonstrate integrity. Act ethically and in alignment with your values, even when no one is watching.

IMPORTANCE TO AN EMPLOYER

An employer places great value on employees who are trustworthy. Trust is the foundation of any successful professional or business relationship. An employee who embodies this trait brings numerous benefits to the workplace. Here are seven reasons why an employer would particularly value an employee who is trustworthy:

1. Reliability: Employers want employees who meet deadlines and fulfill their responsibilities. Reliability fosters a sense of dependability within the workplace and allows the employer to have confidence in the employee's ability to get the job done.

2. Building Teams: Trustworthy individuals contribute to the creation of stronger and more cohesive teams. Team members who trust each other collaborate more effectively and feel comfortable sharing ideas and feedback. This collaborative environment leads to increased productivity, innovation, and overall team success.

3. Enhanced Morale: Trustworthy employees create a sense of safety and security among co-workers. Employees feel more comfortable sharing their thoughts and concerns, which leads to better teamwork, higher job satisfaction, and improved overall morale.

4. Customer Confidence: Trustworthy employees help in building and maintaining customer trust. When customers trust an employee or a company, they are more likely to develop long-term relationships and become loyal customers.

5. Conflict Resolution: Trustworthy employees are better equipped to handle conflicts and difficult situations. Their honesty and transparency fosters open communication, making it easier to address and resolve conflicts in a constructive manner.

6. Ethical Decision-making: Trustworthy employees demonstrate integrity in their decision-making processes. They consider the ethical implications of their actions and will follow company policies. This commitment to ethical values helps organizations maintain a positive reputation and adhere to legal requirements.

7. Leadership Potential: Employers recognize that trustworthy employees inspire and motivate others through their actions. These employees will be entrusted with greater responsibilities and ultimately leadership roles because they will act in the best interest of the organization and its other employees.[0]

EXAMPLES: Trustworthy Core Value Statements

The following are core value statements that you might chose to adopt if being trustworthy was a desired core value.

1. I value trustworthiness above all else and strive to act with honesty and integrity in every aspect of my life.

2. I commit to being a dependable individual, consistently following through on my promises and commitments.

3. I believe in earning and maintaining the trust of others through my words and actions.

4. I will exhibit open and transparent communication in order to demonstrate accountability and authenticity.

5. I respect confidentiality and the privacy of others.

6. I take responsibility for my actions and admit my mistakes, striving to learn and grow from them.

7. I am dedicated to creating a safe environment for those around me, fostering open and supportive communication in order to build strong personal and business relationships.

8. I commit to acting ethically and in accord with my personal core values, even when faced with challenging temptations.

9. I value trustworthiness in leadership and aspire to lead by example, inspiring others to act with honesty and integrity.

10. I will strive to be consistent in all my actions, ensuring that others can rely on me and trust in my character.

MY PERSONAL CORE VALUE – Trustworthiness

Adopt or confirm your personal core value. If being trustworthy is already a core value, or if you want to establish it as a core value, write your personal core value in the space below. You may want to use the examples above as guides to draft your Personal Core Value Statement. Make it short, succinct, and meaningful to you. It should be something you can easily remember.

My *Trustworthiness* core value statement:

_____
_____
_____
_____
_____
_____
_____
_____

DISCUSSIONS AND THOUGHT QUESTIONS

1. Do you believe that most people are trustworthy? Explain.

2. Why do you think trust is considered a vital personal core value in both personal and professional relationships?

3. Recall a time when someone's trustworthiness positively influenced your perception of them. How did it impact your relationship with that person?

4. What are some common consequences of a lack of trustworthiness in personal or professional settings?

5. Did you have to learn to be trusted? How did you learn? Did poor choices ever derail your intentions? Explain.

6. List some things a person would need to do in order to earn your complete trust.

7. What actions or behaviors demonstrate trustworthiness? How do they affect the dynamics within a group or organization?

8. Can you think of any instances when your trustworthiness was tested? Explain. How can one maintain trust in such situations?

9. How does trustworthiness affect your ability to establish and maintain long-lasting relationships?

10. In the Practical Tips section above, which one of the tips do you think would be the most difficult for you? Why?

11. What, if anything, could you share with a friend or group that would help them appreciate the need to be trustworthy?

12. What are potential challenges to being trustworthy? How can these challenges be overcome?

NOTES

I want to do the following:

a. _____

b. _____

c. _____

d. _____

I want to remember:

a. _____

b. _____

c. _____

d. _____

Action Challenge: Identify a relationship where trust could be deepened. What specific, actionable steps can you take this week to demonstrate your trustworthiness and build stronger, more reliable connections with this person?

Chapter 3
Humility

HUMILITY LIFE PRINCIPLE:
I will serve others.

"What kills a skunk is the
publicity it gives itself."
Abraham Lincoln

GENERAL

You may have heard the saying, "Pride goes before a fall." This is actually a proverb from the Bible that is more accurately stated as:

Pride goes before destruction and haughtiness before a fall. Better to live humbly with the poor than to share plunder with the proud. (Proverbs 16:18-19 NLT)

The purpose of this and most other proverbs is to provide experience-based wisdom to help the reader live a better life. Proverbs warn the reader against taking certain actions and then often describe the consequences. In this case the action is pride and the consequence is destruction. This proverb continues with a real life warning by indicating it is better to live humbly (without pride), even to the extent of being poor, and that such a life situation would even be better than having riches (plunder).

In the days of Solomon, this real life explanation referring to "plunder" would have been very meaningful. The message to the reader is that pride can be dangerous and it is better to live a humble life – it is even better to be poor than have the riches produced by pride.

Definitions

Merriam-Webster defines humility as the state of not thinking you are better than others or not exhibiting arrogance. Arrogance describes the practice of acting as if you are better or more important than others. You may think of yourself as entitled. You may even have an attitude of superiority, which often is demonstrated by overbearing words or manners.

Those who lack humility are often conceited and have a very high opinion of themselves and their abilities. Humble people act in a spirit of deference or submission to others. They are not pretentious. Rather, they are modest and unassuming and more concerned about the needs of others than their own desires.

Pride often results from one's belief that he is more important than other people. People with an inordinate level of self-esteem or self-regard often struggle with being humble. Thinking that you are very important can easily lead to arrogance because the line between arrogance and confidence can become very blurred at times.

Humility allows one to consider others in a different light than themselves. The humble person puts the needs of others first and thus does not insist on building himself up in front of others. There is an inherent spirit of submission to the _needs_ of others because the humble person has empathy for other people. It does not mean one is weak. But the humble person does not seek undue attention or recognition for himself.

The focus is on others

When you are around a humble person you will be struck by the concern and care that person exhibits for others compared to themselves. They do not talk about themselves, where they have traveled, who they have met, or what success they have achieved. They do not seem at all interested in talking about themselves, how smart or clever they are, or what exciting thing has happened in their life. Their focus is generally on the achievements of others.

Do you know anyone like this – a truly humble person? It is the neighbor who will mow the grass of an elderly couple before taking care of his own yard. It is the CEO of a large corporation who will do the grilling for his employees at a summer picnic. It is the nurse who goes the extra mile and yet says she could have done so much more.

Humble people want to talk about what others are doing. A story about the seating arrangements at a wedding may be helpful. The story indicates that the humble person would decline to be seated at the head table or at a place of honor. Why? The banquet is not about him, no matter how important or famous he may be. It is about the bride and groom. The focus is on others.

Prideful people on the other hand are primarily interested in themselves. Life revolves around their wants and needs. They have big egos and think they are the most important people in the room. They tend to think they are the center of the universe and they typically have an inflated view of their self-importance.

Humility is an esteemed character trait. It will pay high dividends in relationships. Pride (exalting oneself) will frequently not produce adequate recognition for the arrogant individual. The prideful person will likely suffer because of their arrogant attitudes or lifestyle.

> "*None are so empty as those who are full of themselves*."
> Benjamin Whichcot

Illustration of personal humility

Humility is not a particularly easy personal characteristic to understand. An illustration may be helpful. Sarah was a young woman who was ambitious, hardworking, and driven to succeed. Her business colleagues admired her intelligence and dedication. She was on track to become the youngest partner in her firm's history. However, Sarah's success began to take a toll on her personal life. She became obsessed with her work, working long hours and neglecting her husband and children. Her priorities became skewed, and she lost touch with the things that truly mattered to her.

One day a friend gave her some frank feedback. He told her that her ambition was admirable, but that she needed to take a step back and focus on the bigger life issues. He urged her to cultivate a sense of personal humility and to remember that success is not only just about individual achievement, but also about contributing to the greater good. He advised her to take a serious look at her priorities and what she really wanted in life.

At first, Sarah was very resistant to the advice. She had always prided herself on her ability to achieve personal goals. However, as she thought more about it, she began to think that maybe she needed to reorient some of her priorities.

Over the course of the next year, Sarah worked hard to cultivate a sense of personal humility. She spent more time with her family, volunteered in her community, and began building meaningful relationships with her friends and business colleagues. She came to realize that her life success was not just about her work success, but also about her character and the impact she had on the people around her. She concluded that if she wanted to make her mark in life it was more about how she could positively impact the lives of others rather than being focused totally on her own career success.[1]

BEING WISE IN YOUR OWN EYES

Thinking that you are wise and have great understanding or wisdom can often lead to others thinking you are a fool. Proud attitudes are obvious to all those who associate with people who think they are smarter than the average bear. Fools tend to think of themselves as wise and they often refuse help or advice from others. The consequences are often to their own detriment.

It is often wise to ignore proud people because encouraging them usually leads to increased focus on the wrong things. It becomes even more difficult when you are in a group of arrogant people. Those who think they are wise will consider themselves smarter than the other people in the room. They think they know more and know it better. They often tend to think less of others.

Most experts think that "fixing" someone who is arrogant and prideful is very difficult unless serious professional help is enlisted. Experience demonstrates that it is extremely difficult to transform a fool, particularly when they think they know it all.

> *If I could buy him for what he's worth*
> *and sell him for what he thinks he's worth,*
> *I'd be a very rich man.*

WARNING

Pride leads to difficult times, bumpy relationships, and questionable results. The negative result of excessive pride can be disgrace or embarrassment. Proud people don't want to listen to the advice or opinions of others. Arrogance will usually lead to strife. Strife by definition is created by someone who is very angry or violent in their opposition or disagreement. Simple disagreement and questioning can lead to serious arguments. Arguments or confrontations can often become bitter and contentious.

The resulting dissention can lead to loss of friendships, poor relationships with co-workers, and even fighting or angry words and threats. Trying to give correction or advice to someone who is arrogant can often be very difficult. You will not likely be heard. If you are heard, you usually will be ignored.

The arrogant

When we use the term arrogance we mean: *People who act in an insulting way of thinking or behaving because they feel they are better, smarter, or more important than someone else. They tend to have an attitude of superiority and are often overbearing.*

Arrogant people tend to tune out other people who disagree with them. Suggesting alternatives is often considered a serious rejection of their position. Such people are not open to suggestions. They normally do not react well to advice. Therefore, they have great difficulty working in a team environment. Regardless of the number of people involved in a group, the pride and arrogance of one member will almost always lead to a poor working relationship and a less than desirable result.

Typically arrogant people have difficulties in social and community settings because they are hard to work with. Nobody likes being around people with an attitude. The arrogant will typically not accept warnings or advice that might protect them from trouble. A person's arrogant attitudes will frequently create an atmosphere that causes him to feel he has been put down. This usually occurs because the person experiences a loss of respect, loss of face, or loss of power.

Don't get on your high horse – if you
fall off it's a long way down.

Being obstinate

An ancient term that was frequently used to describe the arrogant and obstinate person was "mocker." These people were usually <u>particularly</u> obnoxious. They could be very obstinate and were not willing to change. They were described as people who were:

- arrogant and filled with excessive pride,
- surrounded by conflict,
- detested by both friends and enemies,
- known to act foolishly,
- incapable of receiving helpful advice,
- refusing instruction or correction, and
- unable to gain knowledge in order to change their behavior.

This is probably a very good summary description of the very prideful person. They are usually not liked by others and they certainly do not appreciate being corrected. Typically mockers thought they were superior to all others and resisted help of any kind.

Fools

Obstinate people may also be referred to as "fools." There are many fools around us but we just don't usually assign this word description to their behavior. A general description of a fool is one who lacks good judgment. They do not normally do what most people think of as right. Their actions or words might be considered silly or ignorant.

The chatter of fools can be very annoying. Seldom do they understand how their words and actions are being received by others. Arrogant speech is not the wise choice if you want to win someone to your side.

Wise and thoughtful words are far more helpful and reasoned actions will avoid the consequences of words or actions that produce angry responses. The wise person will think before he speaks. It is normal to consider how your words will be received by others. Patience and perseverance will usually produce more desirable and helpful responses than aggressive demands that put others on edge.

Avoid egotism

The term "ego" can be described as one's sense of identity. It's the part of our personality that we think of and experience as "self." Some definitions expand ego to include the opinion we have of ourselves. In its purest sense, ego is not a negative. It's our sense of self-worth.

When a person is overly absorbed with himself or has an exaggerated sense of self-importance, we often say he is "egotistical." Thus, egotism becomes a negative description in both social and work environments. Egotism will usually create disruption, anxiety, criticism, and just general unease. Egotism can get in the way of good communication and slow or even stop progress or success.

Egotism can also prevent learning from mistakes. Constructive criticism is generally taboo where egotism reigns. Egotism can prevent any real creative discovery. It is difficult, if not impossible, to deal with people who have inflated egos. Egotism can shade truth in ways that prevent seeing reality.

Relationships suffer when
egotism drives words and actions.

ADVICE

It is certainly easier to be humble and associate with good and caring people than it is to associate with proud and arrogant people. The proud crave to be recognized and applauded. The more attention they receive the more they want. They consider themselves the key to success and often feel they deserve more accolades, more focus, and more reward. They tend to be more interested in the attention and reward they receive than the actual accomplishment.

What does a humble person do when they are associated with the proud and arrogant? Ultimately it's probably best to disassociate or distance yourself from such people. But in their presence you are

54

probably wise to avoid confrontation and allow the proud their moment. You must allow circumstances to dictate how you act. Normally, being publically aggressive toward the arrogant is not the best course of action.

You will ultimately be respected if you can maintain calm while diffusing uncomfortable situations. The humble person will walk away from conflict and environments controlled by people who are openly arrogant. Chalk it up to a learning experience, if necessary, and find better associates and circumstances. In some situations you may need to change friends or jobs.

If you ultimately want to be appreciated for your work or contribution you must put yourself in positive situations. Your reputation is a reflection of respect, esteem, and regard from others produced in part by how you react in uncomfortable situations. You want to live and work in an environment where respect is recognized. This may require you to be humble in awkward circumstances.

Remember, the source of pride and arrogance is the heart. If you want to change or if you want others to change, it will require a change of the heart. That process is neither easy nor quick.

Don't get too big for your own britches.

HUMILITY IN LEADERS

Leaders who are humble servant leaders stand out as the most effective in getting cooperation from followers. People gravitate to leaders who have their best interests at heart. Humble individuals who give thought to the needs and desires of others are very attractive leaders, as well as good friends.

Humility is not necessarily among the traits one considers desired qualities for leadership. That's probably because humility is a very personal characteristic. It is generally not considered in the same category with the more dynamic qualities that reflect traits which are "commanding" in nature.

Humility can go a long way in establishing mutual respect, sincerity, confidence, and trust. Humble leaders recognize that there is always more to learn and that they do not necessarily have all the answers. These attitudes will earn respect from both friends and associates.

Humble leaders who allow subordinates to teach them bring a whole new meaning to being professional.

THE BENEFITS OF HUMILITY

The value of being humble lies in the recognition and acceptance of one's limitations, strengths, and accomplishments without arrogance or excessive pride. It involves maintaining a modest and respectful attitude towards oneself and others.

By acknowledging our own fallibility and showing respect for others, we create an environment of mutual understanding and collaboration. Humility allows us to learn from others, admit mistakes, and continuously strive for self-improvement.

One of the most important and often least recognized benefit of humility is that the humble person is seldom in the middle of conflict. If you often seem to be in the middle of chaos or discord, you might examine closely why such dissent seems to exist around your work or relationships. Self-evaluation is always a good place to start.

Humility cannot solve all conflict but it can often be the catalyst to resolving a situation quickly. Some of the obvious benefits of being humble include:

- You are respected and honored by both leaders and followers.
- You receive rewards and opportunities before others because of strong relationships.
- You live and work in a more "gentle" environment.
- You have less stress and anxiety.
- You learn from your mistakes and embrace new ideas.
- You are less prone to want to prove yourself right.
- You have inner peace and contentment.

Remember, you reap what you sow.
Sow the seeds of humility.

CONCLUSION

A man who is wise in his own eyes is a fool! Fools think they are always right and their way is the only way. If one is wise it will be known and talked about by others – only a fool thinks it is necessary to tell the world about his accomplishments. Pride is almost always detestable to others! These are very strong words, but true.

Proud speech or verbal arrogance produces stress and negative responses. People simply do not want to hear about your "great accomplishments." The truth that the proud person never understands is that others know when one has done well or been successful. They do not need to be told about it.

Humility will produce respect and reward on its own. There is no reason to broadcast good results to others. Others will do that if it is warranted. If you want to develop humility in your life, practice gratitude, listen to the needs of others, and try to help others succeed.

PRACTICAL TIPS FOR BEING HUMBLE

1.   Don't talk about yourself.
2.   If you must talk about your work don't be overly dramatic.
3.   Seek the thoughts and opinions of others.
4.   Don't take all the credit yourself. Share it with others.
5.   Be professional. Generate respect, not fear.
6.   Be calm and quell turmoil.
7.   Admit your mistakes.
8.   Give credit to others for their contributions.
9.   Practice gratitude by expressing appreciation for the people, experiences, and opportunities in your life
10. Serve others. Look for opportunities to help and support others without expecting anything in return.

EXAMPLES: Humility Core Value Statements

Here are some examples of personal core value statements for humility that are focused on various aspects of being humble.

1. I will appreciate my strengths and accomplishments without seeking attention or validation.

2. I will prioritize humility by willingly serving others.

3. I will embody humility by readily admitting my mistakes, and taking responsibility for my words and actions.

4. I will practice humility by acknowledging and highlighting the contributions and achievements of others.

5. I will exhibit humility by valuing diverse perspectives and being receptive to different ideas and opinions.

6. I will empower others and create a collaborative and inclusive environment where everyone's contributions are valued.

MY PERSONAL CORE VALUE – Humility

If being humble is already a core value or if you want to establish it as a core value, write your personal core value in the space below. You may want to use the examples above to craft your personal version of this core value. Make it short, succinct, and meaningful to you.

Humility:

_____
_____
_____
_____
_____
_____

DISCUSSION AND THOUGHT QUESTIONS

1. How would you define humility, and why do you think it is an important personal core value?

2. Reflect on a time when you witnessed someone displaying humility. How did their attitude impact you or others?

3. In what ways do you think humility can enhance your relationships with others?

4. Think about a situation in which humility could have helped resolve a conflict or improved communication. How might a humble approach have made a difference?

5. Which one of the "Practical Tips" above would be the most difficult for you? Why? Which tip would be the best and most effective for you? Why?

6. What do you think are some of the biggest challenges to being humble in today's world?

7. How should you respond when you are complimented?

8. Reflect on the role of humility in handling success.

9. Share an example in which a lack of humility led to negative consequences or strained relationships?

10. Reflect on or share your own experiences with humility and the impact it has had on your relationships.

NOTES
I want to do or remember the following:

a. _____
b. _____
c. _____
d. _____
e. _____

Action Challenge: Think about a recent interaction where you could have been more humble. What did you learn from that experience, and how can you apply that lesson to future interactions to foster better understanding and growth?

Chapter 4
Forgiveness

FORGIVENESS LIFE PRINCIPLE:
I will not hold grudges.

"Forgiving isn't something you do for someone else.
It's something you do for yourself. It's saying 'You're not
important enough to have a stranglehold on me.'
It's saying, 'You don't get to trap me in the past.
I am worthy of a future'."
Jodi Picoult

GENERAL

Forgiveness is a decision. It is a voluntary act that you make for *yourself*. It is not something you necessarily do for someone else. The fundamental need for forgiveness resides within each of us. It releases us from the need to harbor revenge or nurse hurt. Please read that last sentence again. *It releases us from the need to deal with the continuing experience of the hurt.*

The paragraph above summarizes the foundational purpose of this chapter and this subject. We forgive in order to lift the burden of carrying around heavy baggage that can weigh us down, wear us out, and even destroy our lives. We forgive because the weight of grudges, thoughts of revenge, feelings of sadness, and the ongoing emotional stress is debilitating.

How can we forgive if the hurt is great? We simply decide to. It is that simple and that hard. The key to deciding to forgive is to understand that the act is done to benefit yourself, not to excuse the behavior of another. It is simply the act of heart and mind to relieve yourself from the mental and emotional burden of the relentless thoughts and hurt of a situation that cannot be undone.

> *"Forgiveness liberates the victim.*
> *It's a gift you give yourself."*
> T.D. Jakes

The above quote by T.D. Jakes accurately states that the act of forgiving does not excuse the act causing the hurt. It is an action that frees the victim from the ongoing mental misery of dealing with the situation. The one causing the hurt is not exonerated or relieved of responsibility, but the victim is liberated from the continuing need to remain in a state of anger.

We can tell a perpetrator they are forgiven but not excused. We can decide not to hold a grudge or hate that person without forgetting the event. We forgive, but that does not necessarily mean we forget. Depending on the situation our relationship with the other party may change even though we have truly forgiven the individual.

Some of you may be thinking that this is just pie-in-the-sky talk and no one can really forgive a serious hurt. You may feel that In order for justice to be done it is necessary for the perpetrator to experience a similar hurt. Why? Why do you think that an "eye-for-an-eye" mentality is the solution to the problem? Stop for a moment and think if such a physical solution would really <u>solve the problem</u>. What is the real issue and what would really fix that problem?

Regardless of how much you might want another to suffer in the same way you are suffering, what would that accomplish? Think for a moment about two possible solutions for the future. One is that the perpetrator is suffering on the same level as yourself and you both are miserable and living troubled lives. Or, that you truly forgive someone and live a positive and fruitful life. Do you really care how the perpetrator is living as long as you are living a good life? Your first and perhaps only concern should be your own mental health. You need <u>not</u> be concerned about the welfare of the one that caused the hurt.

I have somewhat overstated the foregoing situation because it is important that you begin with the understanding that forgiveness begins with you. You must be right with yourself before you can do much for others. Should you forgive another person if they ask – certainly! Should you want them to suffer as you are suffering – no. Should you be concerned for the health of the perpetrator – yes. Should you do what you can to restore the relationship? Probably!

But all that doesn't change the fact that you need to fix yourself before you can be much help to anyone else. In this situation that means you must forgive.

My responsibility is to forgive others when they have hurt me. I should also apologize to those I have offended. I can ask for forgiveness from those I have offended, but how they respond is totally outside of my control. In the same way, I cannot control whether my offer of forgiveness is accepted or rejected. I cannot control whether the offending person apologizes or not. I can only control my own responses. Jonathon Huie has said, "Forgive others, not because they deserve forgiveness, but because you deserve peace."

In some cases the forgiveness must be directed toward oneself. It can be challenging to forgive yourself if you are the cause of someone else suffering. Forgiving yourself can be extremely difficult, but is absolutely necessary to live a life of contentment.

"How unhappy is he who
cannot forgive himself."
Publius Syrus

Mary Johnson and Oshea Israel

Personal forgiveness is a powerful tool that not only benefits the person being forgiven, but also the person doing the forgiving. An example of the importance of personal forgiveness comes from the story of Mary Johnson and Oshea Israel.

In 1993, Oshea Israel shot and killed Mary Johnson's son, Laramiun Byrd, during an argument at a party. Johnson was devastated by the loss of her son and struggled with anger and grief for many years. However, in 2005, Johnson attended a mediation session with Israel and was moved by his apology and expression of remorse for his actions. Over time, Johnson and Israel developed a unique relationship based on forgiveness and understanding. Johnson even went so far as to help Israel find a job and housing after he was released from prison. The two now give talks together about the power of forgiveness and the importance of redemption.[2]

Their story is a powerful reminder of the healing power of forgiveness, and how it can transform even the most difficult situations into opportunities for growth and compassion. Forgiveness is not easy, but the rewards of letting go of anger and resentment can be immeasurable.

> *"Forgiveness is not to give the other person peace.*
> *Forgiveness is for you. Take that opportunity."*
> Mackenzie Phillips

RECOVERY PROCESS

If you were God you could forget completely the offense that was committed. However you are not God and depending on your personality, you may find it very difficult to put negative and unhealthy thoughts aside. Even though you may not take any overt action against the offender, you may not want to see them, talk to them, or associate with them in any way. That is understandable and not necessarily inappropriate. It all depends on the circumstances. You may not actively hold a grudge but you find it very difficult to be around that person because they are a reminder of the offense.

I wish I could tell you that there was a button to push that would make the hurt go away. Unfortunately that is not possible. Resolution will require two important actions. One is out of your control: time. Time will dull the hurt and is often needed in order for you to mentally and emotional deal with the situation.

The other action is a true desire to forgive and move on. This may require meditation, prayer, or talking about it. Talking about it with others may prove to be very helpful. The others could be family members, friends, business associates, or professionals. All of these sources of help will require that you describe your feelings. It is often extremely helpful to verbalize the situation.

Are you mad, sad, or glad? How are you really feeling? Talking out loud about the situation will often help you crystalize your thinking and understand how you are really feeling. If you are seriously angry it may take some time before you can rationally deal with your feelings.

If your emotions are in check and you can think clearly you can begin to understand that your forgiveness isn't about the offense or the offending party, but how you want to personally deal with the situation. Harboring hate is debilitating. This is why forgiveness is for your benefit, not for the offending party.

> *"I learned a long time ago that some people*
> *would rather die than forgive. It's a strange truth,*
> *but forgiveness is a painful and difficult process.*
> *It's not something that happens overnight.*
> *It's an evolution of the heart."*
> Sue Monk Kidd

If you forgive others their offenses, they are most likely going to forgive you when you offend them. If you apologize and ask for forgiveness for your offenses you are likely to receive it. Silence can be the big killer preventing forgiveness in relationships.

We cannot go through this life without forgiveness. We all will offend someone at some time and others will offend us. The cause can range from the silly to the serious. Regardless of the nature of the offense, the sooner forgiveness is granted and accepted, the sooner life will get back to normal.

Forgiveness may require a great deal of strength, trust, or confidence. It may not be easy, even if it is only a minor offense.

Thomas Szasz has said, "The stupid neither forgive nor forget; the naïve forgive and forget; and the wise forgive but do not forget." This is a very accurate summary of the reactions to events that cause hurt. Why? The purpose of forgiving is to start over or wipe the slate clean so that your life can continue under generally normal circumstances. If you do not forgive, the burden of the hurt will last a long time, maybe forever. That is not in your best interest.

If you take the step of granting forgiveness and then actually forget about what happened, you are inviting the recurrence of the event and could experience the hurt again. It is important to forgive but not really forget. If you don't forget, it is much easier to prevent the hurt from occurring again.

What happens if you do not forgive? It's possible to ignore an incident if it is of relatively little significance. It is more likely to cause stress and painful memories if the situation is not resolved. If forgiveness does not occur within a reasonable amount of time the mind will begin to build space for a grudge that can turn into thoughts of revenge. Hateful thoughts or plans for revenge will generally cause more harm than good. They will not relieve the pain of the offense and they are not enjoyable to carry around.

The old saying that forgiveness can set you free is true. Forgiveness can set you free! It will release you from the bondage of pain and resentment that can become very heavy weights in your life. The wise person will recognize that the emotional baggage is not healthy and provides no real solution to the hurt. Forgiving but not forgetting is the best option that allows you to move on with life.

You might ask if someone continually offends you, how many times should you forgive the offense. The very easy answer is however many times it takes. I can see the smirk on some of your faces! Yes, I know this can be difficult and trying, and maybe even impossible in your lifetime. But just remember, the act of forgiving the offense is for your benefit, not for the benefit of the offender.

Again, this does not mean you like, condone, or approve of the offender or their behavior. It does mean you absolve the event or the perpetrator from the consequences they may encounter. In fact there may be serious consequences to the offending party. You may need to establish certain boundaries for your interactions with certain people who don't demonstrate an ability to be trustworthy. Protect yourself!

"It's not an easy journey, to get to a place
where you forgive people.
But it is such a powerful place,
because it frees you."
Tyler Perry

YOU MUST ASK OR TELL

You might want to keep the forgiveness between you, yourself, and your journal. That is not the best solution because unless you verbally express your forgiveness to the perpetrator or the appropriate people, you may always feel you never really granted the forgiveness.

You are not necessarily required to tell someone they are forgiven – in fact they may not even know you are offended. Assuming all parties know about the situation, why would you need to tell the other party that you have forgiven them? There are a number of reasons:

- for your peace of mind,
- to relieve stress and tension,
- for your satisfaction,
- to free yourself from guilt,
- it will go a long way in restoring a relationship, or
- it can head off possible feelings for revenge.

If you want forgiveness from a party you have offended, you will most likely have to ask for it. Regardless, you should apologize for your poor behavior and do it as quickly as possible. The longer the delay the more difficult it becomes to resolve all the feelings and emotions that are created around the event by all parties.

What kinds of things make you feel that you should be asked for your forgiveness? Often it is anything that makes you feel bad and certainly when some kind of hurt or suffering has occurred. But it can also be for something you did not do but are on the receiving end of the blame, even though you had no control over the situation.

Sometimes it is for something that is very unimportant and the negative fuss becomes blown way out of proportion. Restoration is paramount. Quickly getting to the resolution stage can often prevent little things from becoming big things.

"Always forgive your enemies,
nothing annoys them so much."
Oscar Wilde

GRUDGES AND REVENGE

How should you react when someone asks you to be forgiven? Take the high ground and provide your forgiveness and mean it. You have nothing to gain by holding a grudge, particularly if the person involved is family, a coworker, or close friend. Holding grudges is often known only by the one holding the grudge.

Living in a constant state of unforgiveness can destroy one's peace and contentment. Life becomes a battleground and anxiety and stress can reign. Do you know anyone who has carried a grudge and is unwilling to give it up? Their lives become consumed with the event and can be ruled by the mental anguish associated with the actual hurt, or be ruled by an inflated hurt far beyond reality. They cannot think about anything else and they become consumed to the point that their life revolves around that event. This describes an extreme situation but there can be many lesser realities that are just as debilitating.

How do you feel when you want to pay somebody back for an offense they initiated? Probably not very good! You might even describe yourself as feeling terrible. Feeling that you have been offended to the degree that you would consider revenge creates an extremely high degree of stress. You typically can't get it off your mind. Often your work or responsibilities are negatively impacted because your mind is occupied with thoughts about the offense.

Unforgiveness produces excessive
sorrow, hurt, and sadness, usually for both parties!

RECONCILIATION

The purpose of forgiveness is to provide restoration and reconciliation in a relationship. Separation will continue in a relationship that has been ruptured by an offense until one of the parties initiates discussion aimed at resolution. You will continue to be alienated from the other party until you can achieve some level of reconciliation.

Restoration cannot be achieved until both parties agree they are not going to hold the offense against the other. In most cases the damage has been done and cannot be corrected or undone. It is simply a matter of deciding to forgive and move on. The offense did occur and did exist, but the parties agree that mistakes happen and such offense is going to be put aside and not be allowed to negatively impact the relationship. That is grace.

> *"Forgiveness is not an occasional act,*
> *it is a constant attitude."*
> Martin Luther King Jr.

PRACTICAL TIPS

Here are some simple and easy-to-implement tips for demonstrating or practicing forgiveness:

1. Reflect on your own past mistakes and instances where you were forgiven and how it made you feel. What would you have changed?

2. Understand that forgiveness is a choice and make a conscious decision to release grudges and resentment. Do you have such a situation in your life today?

3. Practice self-forgiveness by releasing any guilt or shame.

4. Communicate openly and honestly with the person you want to forgive, allowing for dialogue to begin.

5. Release the need for an apology from the other person.

6. Give yourself time to heal before attempting to forgive.

7. Seek support from trusted friends or family who can provide guidance and perspective.

8. Engage in self-care activities that promote relaxation like exercise or spending time in nature.

9. Write a forgiveness letter, even if you don't send it. This can help you process your emotions and gain clarity.

10. Focus on the positive aspects of the person or situation, recognizing that everyone is flawed.

11. Determine what lessons you learned from the experience.

12. Release the emotional burden associated with the offense.

"True forgiveness is when you can say,
'Thank you for that experience'."
Oprah Winfrey

CONCLUSION

We have discussed a number of benefits above as we described the need to forgive. Forgiveness will help reduce stress and anxiety by releasing the body's natural stress hormones. Your physical health can be improved. Forgiveness has been linked to a number of physical health benefits, including improved cardiovascular health, reduced blood pressure, and a stronger immune system. Lastly, your contentment and well-being can be increased.

Forgiveness can be a difficult process, especially if the offense was severe or if you have been hurt multiple times by the same person. Patience and perseverance can serve you well, but forgiveness is a journey, not a destination. It takes time to process the pain and hurt caused by the offense.

Forgiveness does not mean that you condone the offense or that you are weak. It simply means that you are choosing to let go of the anger and resentment so that you can move on with your life.

EXAMPLES: Forgiveness Core Value Statements

1. I value forgiveness as a guiding principle in my life, choosing to release resentment and embrace compassion.

2. Forgiveness is at the core of who I am. I will let go of past hurts and cultivate peace within myself.

3. I believe in the power of forgiveness to break the cycle of pain and foster healing and reconciliation.

4. Forgiveness is a value I will use to reconcile relationships.

5. Forgiveness is a cornerstone of my relationships in order to foster personal connections and strong friendships.

6. Forgiveness is my anchor in for life's relational challenges.

7. I embrace forgiveness and reconciliation as methods to resolve hurts and affronts. I will not hold grudges.

8. I commit to practicing forgiveness towards myself and others, recognizing we are all imperfect.

9. I value forgiveness as a means to restore harmony and cultivate authentic connections in my relationships.

10. Forgiveness is my compass in navigating conflicts, guiding me to seek resolution, understanding, and reconciliation.

MY PERSONAL CORE VALUE – Forgiveness

Adopt or confirm your core value. If forgiveness is already a core value, or if you want to establish it as a core value, write your personal core value in the space below. You may want to use the examples above as guides to draft your Personal Core Value Statement. Make it short, succinct, and meaningful to you. Something you can easily remember.

Forgiveness:

_____
_____
_____
_____
_____
_____
_____

DISCUSSION AND THOUGHT QUESTIONS

1. What does forgiveness mean to you personally? How would you define it in your own words?

2. Have you ever experienced the power of forgiveness? If so, could you share an example and explain how it impacted you?

3. In your opinion, what are some of the main benefits or positive outcomes of practicing forgiveness?

4. Is there anyone in your life you need to forgive? Are you carrying baggage you need to shed by giving the problem up or do you need to tell someone you forgive them?

5. Bryant McGill has said, "There is no love without forgiveness, and there is no forgiveness without love." What do you think he means? Do you agree?

6. Can you think of a situation in which holding onto a grudge or refusing to forgive had negative consequences for someone involved? What lessons can be learned from that situation?

7. Can forgiveness be seen as a sign of strength rather than weakness? Why or why not?

8. Is forgiveness a one-time event or a continuous process? Can you think of any examples where forgiveness requires ongoing effort?

9. Are there any situations in which forgiveness may not be appropriate or necessary? When might it be healthier to set boundaries or distance oneself from someone instead?

10. How does forgiving oneself differ from forgiving others? Are there unique challenges or considerations involved in self-forgiveness?

NOTES

I want to do the following:

a. _____

b. _____

c. _____

d. _____

I want to remember:

a. _____

b. _____

c. _____

d. _____

Action Challenge: Consider a past hurt that you're still holding onto. Write a letter (that you don't have to send) to the person who caused the hurt, expressing your feelings and then consciously choosing to forgive them, releasing yourself from the burden of resentment.

Chapter 5
Accountability

ACCOUNTABILITY LIFE PRINCIPLE:
I will take responsibility.

"The world needs more people who are willing
to be responsible for their actions, and less who
are willing to blame others for their mistakes."
Unknown

GENERAL

Our definition of personal accountability is the willingness to take ownership of one's actions and outcomes. It includes accepting responsibility for the consequences of what you do and say, whether it is under your control or not. People who are personally accountable do not blame others or external factors for their mistakes. Instead, they take responsibility and work to correct their errors in order to achieve their objectives. Personal accountability is important in both personal and professional settings as it enables individuals to build trust and foster positive relationships.

Accountability means that you accept responsibility for your actions or those of your group. The group may be a family, work team, or a community organization. It may mean taking responsibility for falling short of goals or for not fulfilling promises. Taking responsibility for poor decisions is a characteristic of good leaders. It demonstrates you are willing to stand up for your friends or associates. Subordinates will make mistakes! It is often the leader who accepts responsibility for the group rather than pointing out the mistakes of a team member.

In today's world everyone wants to find someone to blame. But people of high character do not cast blame and look for scapegoats. For example, if you listen to the interviews on Sunday afternoon following an NFL football game, you will almost always hear the losing quarterback taking the blame for the loss.

While everyone should be accountable, it is particularly important for leaders. A leader's lack of accountability can negatively influence an entire team and seriously impact results. A culture of accountability allows everyone in a group to understand what is expected. It also allows leaders to expect and demand excellence.

Developing accountability may require making changes in behavior or mindset. We will not focus in this chapter on how to prevent poor or bad results. The focus will be on what we do after the results or consequences have occurred and we have participated in or been responsible for the result. How do you act or react to your mistakes or misunderstandings? A wrong or undesirable result has occurred and the question is, "How do you respond?" Or, if a good result has occurred, who takes credit?

At one end of the spectrum we take immediate responsibility for the blunder and at the other end we totally ignore the result or blame someone else for the mistake. If the result is good we can take immediate credit or give recognition to the team. The possible responses can be endless depending on our mindset.

There are a number of things to consider when faced with errors or mistakes. How quickly do you respond? Do you engage the situation immediately or do you let it simmer for a while? What do you say or do about the mistake and do you respond privately or publically? One important consideration may be, "Will public knowledge hurt or elevate others?" If the result is bad, how serious is the problem and what are the possible solutions? Who are the first people that need to know about the situation?

> *"Accountability is the glue that ties commitment to the result."*
> Bob Proctor

Illustration

This is a story about John who is a talented football player. He had a reputation for being unreliable because he often skipped practice and neglected his responsibilities both on and off the field. Despite this, his coach believed in his potential and continued to give him chances he probably did not deserve.

A few months back the team was preparing for an important game and John was missing. His absence was felt, and the team struggled without him. It was later discovered that he had skipped practice to attend a party and had been picked up by the police.

The consequences of his actions were severe. He was suspended from the team and ultimately missed out on a potential college scholarship. It was a wake-up call for him, and he realized that he needed to take responsibility for his actions if he wanted to recover from this serious situation. He worked hard to make things right. He apologized to his team and his coach. He started showing up early to practice and putting in extra effort. His hard work paid off and he was reinstated to the team.

John finally realized that his actions didn't just affect him but also those around him. He understood that if he wanted to achieve his goals, he needed to make choices that aligned with his personal goals and those of the team.

This story is an illustration that personal accountability is crucial in all areas of life. When we take ownership of our decisions we can achieve greater things and hopefully inspire others to do the same.[1]

> *"True accountability only exists when people take ownership of their responsibilities and results."*
> Henry J. Evans

TAKE RESPONSIBILITY

When we are accountable, we take responsibility for our actions and the results whether individually or as a member of a group. We all have a tendency to avoid poor outcomes. Without thinking we may lie about the facts or attempt to shift blame because we want to avoid the embarrassment of admitting we made a mistake.

The problem with this approach is that it becomes more and more difficult to maintain the lies to avoid responsibility. When the truth is discovered, the consequences are usually far worse than would have been experienced if fault had been admitted at the beginning.

Rather than focusing on the mistake or problem, the best course of action is to concentrate on the solution. How do you fix the problem? It may be a very simple solution and before the event turns into a disaster, the problem is resolved. If the situation is not simple then it is probably even more important to attack the problem immediately. Wasting time trying to avoid blame may cause the situation to become worse. So, regardless of the size of the problem, your first thoughts should be directed to solutions and fixes, not on trying to cover it up or fix blame.

If you think back over the history of major public cover-ups, it is obvious that if those responsible for the problem had come forward and admitted the error or mistake, the entire situation may never have reached the public outcry that ultimately occurred. The cover-up can often have more dire consequences than the actual offense.

Take responsibility. Accountability can
prevent a world of hurt!

MISTAKES!

What happens when we make a mistake? A mistake is not the end of the world – it's a mistake, not a death sentence! If we make a wrong choice, we should rethink the issue and select another solution. We all make mistakes. The real challenge in life is how we respond.

Statistics say that successful entrepreneurs on the average have seven failed business ventures before they finally succeed. What does this tell us? If something is not working or the desired result is not occurring, stop and change direction. Try something new.

Not every choice we make will be the right decision. Expect some failures in life and don't be overwhelmed if what you choose does not work out as you expect the first time. If the choice was wrong or ill-advised, fix it! If necessary, move on and find another solution.

George Bernard Shaw said, "We are made wise not by the recollection of our past, but by the responsibility for our future." Beware of false knowledge; it is more dangerous than ignorance. Success does not consist in never making mistakes but in never making the same one a second time.

In other words, we should learn from our mistakes. At any point in our existence the most important time frame is the future because it is the only timeline we can influence. We cannot go back and undo errors, but we can fix them or prevent them from happening in the future.

BE FAIR AND JUST

Fairness and justice are not directly related to accountability but they are worth a brief mention here. Regardless of who may be responsible for an error, those persons must be treated with fairness and justice. That includes you as well. Fixing problems should not include harsh treatment of those responsible. The focus should be on correcting the problem and taking steps to prevent the situation from recurring.

Responsible people and particularly good leaders exhibit fairness when dealing with others in their sphere of influence. Everyone should accept their share of any blame. People should not be excused because they made an innocent mistake or didn't know what they were doing. Someone is responsible.

A problem may have occurred because somebody was not well-trained. That result is on both the individual and the leaders. In a group environment, everyone accepts his share of the responsibility.

Fairness is often central to the way employees or friends expect to be treated. They will in turn treat others the way they are treated in both social and work environments. Treating some people better than others will cause jealousy and produce claims of favoritism. Workers, in particular, have rebelled or quit when they perceived they were not treated fairly or with justice.

This means that correction or "blame" must be administered and communicated fairly and clearly. A leader cannot fire one employee for dishonesty (for example, stealing company supplies) and only warn another. Good employees should be rewarded more than poor employees. Inept or disruptive employees must be let go.

The same is true for friends and associates. If you do not respect your friends, you may not have many friends, and those you do have may not consider you a real friend. The fallout for a lack of respect can last a long time, sometimes forever!

WHO TO BLAME

Blame is a big concern for many people today. When something bad happens, the first reaction by many is to find someone to blame. Our culture no longer seems to accept the concept of an "accident." It's become the mindset to assign blame and "make someone pay." We have forgotten the definition of an accident, which is an unplanned or unforeseen occurrence. It is no longer acceptable to merely restore the victim to their position before an accident. Rather we think we must extract a huge monetary punishment from the other party.

Some of us react in illogical ways to consequences. The most illogical is the person who totally ignores the obvious dangers of what they are about to do and then rather than accepting the consequences, casts blame on others. They become angry or embarrassed and attempt to find someone or something to blame in order to take the attention off their own poor judgment.

Taking responsibility for mistakes, misunderstandings, or accidents is becoming a lost art because many children have been raised to believe they do not have to suffer consequences. If the result of some action is not good they expect someone else will fix it and the boss, parent, or coach has no right to hold them responsible.

Admitting mistakes and being accountable is a characteristic of those who are seeking to live life at a high ethical level.

> *"As we must account for every idle word,*
> *so must we account for every idle silence."*
> Benjamin Franklin

SILENCE

The above quote by Ben Franklin raises a very important concept in the area of responsibility. It is simply not acceptable to remain silent when our knowledge can fix or prevent a problem. If we are going to be held accountable for our actions, we will also be held accountable for our silence if it causes negative consequences.

Instead of assuming responsibility by taking action some people wait for someone else to do it in the hope of avoiding negative fallout. That seldom works and usually results in more severe consequences. People with ethical core values will not remain silent when speaking up will fix a problem or prevent some negative result.

PRACTICAL TIPS

Here are several suggestions on how you might develop this trait:

1. Accept responsibility for your decisions, good and bad.

2. Be transparent about your actions. Don't lie or make excuses.

3. Maintain open and honest communication with others, especially when things go wrong.

4. Acknowledge your errors without making excuses and be willing to learn from them.

5. Embrace constructive criticism and use it as an opportunity for personal development.

6. Concentrate on finding solutions and contributing to problem-solving efforts.

7. Work well with others, share information, and support team members in achieving shared goals.

8. Consistently deliver on your commitments and build a reputation for being dependable.

Take responsibility and be accountable!

REMEMBER

Know and trust yourself and what you can do. Establish core values that represent high character and take responsibility for your words and actions. Those values, if you hold to them, will not fail you. Stress, family, and work responsibilities can impact your desire to maintain your core values. It can be easy to lose focus and put too much value on self and not enough on matters of truth, integrity, or justice.

Sometime we can make choices impulsively rather than intentionally. When we do this we need to slow down and consider who we are and what we want to be. Impulsive decisions can cause a lifetime of regret. Keeping our core values and goals in clear sight is important and can prevent us from making impulsive choices.

Don't succumb to peer pressure when difficulties occur. If you connect to the core values you have established, the answers to many problems will tend to become obvious.

IMPORTANCE TO AN EMPLOYER

Accountable employees create trust within the workplace. Employers can rely on them to fulfill their work responsibilities. By taking ownership of their actions, employees create a reputation for dependability and reliability. They are more likely to meet deadlines, follow through on commitments, and ensure that tasks are completed to the best of their ability. This level of dependability allows employers to delegate important tasks with confidence.

Accountable employees also tend to have good problem-solving skills. They approach challenges with a proactive mindset and seek effective solutions instead of dwelling on the problem itself. Rather than shifting blame or making excuses, they focus on identifying and addressing the root cause of issues. This proactive approach not only helps them overcome obstacles but also contributes to a more productive and efficient work environment.

Employees with a strong sense of accountability generally demonstrate a commitment to continuous learning and growth. They are receptive to feedback, whether it is positive or critical, and use it as an opportunity to improve their skills and performance. Their willingness to take responsibility for their actions contributes to personal development and professional growth.

Such employees tend to excel in teamwork. They recognize the impact of their actions on others and actively contribute to a positive work culture. By openly communicating and accepting responsibility they foster an environment of cooperation. Such teamwork enhances productivity and leads to better problem-solving and innovation.

Accountable employees adhere to professional standards, follow organizational policies, and act in the best interests of the company. This approach to work builds a reputation for the employee as someone who can be trusted to make sound and ethical decisions. Such employees are typically more likely to be promoted into leadership positions.[0]

EXAMPLES: Accountability Core Value Statements

Here are some sample core value statements that you might choose if you were adopting accountability as a personal core value:

1. I value accountability and take full ownership of my decisions.

2. I prioritize personal responsibility in all my commitments.

3. Accountability is at the center of my core values.

4. I embrace accountability as a key component of my personal and professional growth.

5. I will be accountable for my mistakes, openly admit them, and actively learn from them.I will practice accountability by seeking solutions rather than dwelling on the problems or casting blame.

6. Accountability is the foundation of my work ethic.

7. I will take full responsibility for the impact of my words and actions.

MY PERSONAL CORE VALUE – Accountability

Adopt or confirm your core value. If accountability is already a core value, or if you want to establish it as a core value, write your personal core value statement in the space below. You may want to use the examples above as guides to draft your Personal Core Value

Statement. Make it short, succinct, and meaningful to you. Something you can easily remember.

Accountability:

_____

_____

_____

_____

_____

_____

DISSCUSSION AND THOUGHT QUESTIONS

1. What does personal accountability mean to you? How do you think it contributes to your personal growth and development?

2. How do you practice personal accountability in your (a) family, (b) faith, or (c) career?

3. What do you think are the most important benefits of being personally accountable?

4. What are some barriers for you in being personally accountable?

5. How do you typically handle situations when you fail to meet your expectations or the requirements of the situation?

6. How do you deal with constructive feedback or advice from family, friends, or co-workers about your behavior or performance?

7. How does stress from being accountable impact you? How do you deal with it?

8. How do you balance being personally accountable with being compassionate and forgiving when others fail?

9. Do you help or encourage others to be more accountable? Why? Why not? If so, how?

10. How do you handle situations when others who created or caused a problem refuse to be accountable and try to blame you or others for a negative outcome?

11. What are some examples of personal accountability you face in everyday life, and how do they impact your relationships?

12. How does personal accountability contribute to ethical decision-making and integrity in your life?

NOTES

I want to do the following:

a. _____

b. _____

c. _____

d. _____

I want to remember:

a. _____

b. _____

c. _____

d. _____

Action Challenge: Identify an area in your life where you've been avoiding responsibility. What specific steps can you take this week to own your actions, learn from your mistakes, and create a plan for moving forward with greater accountability?

Chapter 6
Authenticity

AUTHENTICITY LIFE PRINCIPLE:
I will be real, genuine, and sincere.

An authentic person is one
willing to be himself in all circumstances.

GENERAL

Personal authenticity is a concept that has different meanings and interpretations in different areas of life. In general, it means being true to a given standard, like your own core values. There is the underlying concept that an authentic person adheres to his beliefs even when there is pressure to compromise his standards.

Being authentic is being honest with yourself and others. It means that your actions match your words. You do not waiver in the face of conflicting pressures for conformity. Merriam-Webster describes personal authenticity as being true to one's own beliefs or character.

Why authenticity is important

Being authentic can have many benefits for your well-being, such as self-esteem and coping with challenges or difficulties. It can enhance your well-being and how well you perform responsibilities and assigned tasks. It can impact how well you engage with people and activities. Are you fully involved and committed, or are you only superficially involved in a task?

Being authentic can help you build trust and respect. It is also a building block to integrity because you do the right thing and take responsibility for your words and actions.

Being authentic is also associated with being autonomous and purposeful in what you are doing. You may even be considered unique, which will attract you to a certain portion of society looking to avoid the mundane. Being authentic can produce the view that you are trustworthy because you are not fake or phony. People see through an insincere personality very quickly.

> *"When you show up authentic, you create the*
> *space for others to do the same. Walk in your truth."*
> Anonymous

How authenticity is demonstrated

Authenticity is characterized by self-awareness, transparency, and being genuine. Authentic people are sincere and true to themselves and their values. They will admit when they are wrong. Here are a several good examples of how to demonstrate authenticity:

- *Be true to yourself.* Authentic people are not afraid to be themselves, even if it means being different. They are not afraid to show their emotions or admit when they are wrong.

- *Be transparent.* Authentic people are honest and open with others. They are likely to share their thoughts and feelings and they are willing to ask for help when they need it.

- *Be genuine.* Authentic people are not phony or manipulative. They are genuine and sincere and they generally act in the best interests of their friends or co-workers.

Authenticity is an important quality for any person and it is particularly helpful for leaders who want to build trust and rapport with their employees or team. When leaders are authentic their followers are more likely to trust, respect, and be inspired by them.

> *"When you are authentic,*
> *you create a certain energy.*
> *People want to be around you*
> *because you are unique."*
> Andie MacDowell

HOW TO DEVELOP AUTHENTICITY

If you do not have the natural inclination to be open and transparent, you may need to work at being authentic. Here are a few ways to develop personal authenticity:

Reflect on your lifestyle. What are the principles and core values that guide your life? Do you rely on these values in decision-making? What are your personal objectives and goals? Do your choices align with your values? What are you passionate about? Do your values reflect your passions?

Observe yourself. Learn to examine your thoughts, feelings, motives, and behaviors. Do you know your bias? Try to observe when you are being authentic and when you are not. What triggers you to put on a mask so others won't know you? How do you react to both success and failure?

Challenge your doubts. Sometimes we fail to be authentic because we doubt ourselves or our abilities. We may be afraid of rejection or failure. We may have inner messages that make us feel unworthy or inadequate. Challenge these thoughts and feelings and replace them with affirmations. There is nothing wrong with doubt. We all have some doubt, but don't allow it to drive your life.

Develop courage. Being authentic can be frightening, especially when it means going against the norm or risking conflict. Being true to yourself can be liberating and empowering. If you need courage, begin by taking small steps. Seek support from others if you need it.

Talk to yourself. There are times you may want to please others rather than being your true to yourself. You may have to talk to yourself – maybe with some harsh words! Compromise may be appropriate, but don't be untrue to your core values simply to avoid conflict.

Act accordingly. Once you know what is important and right, align your actions with your values. This means being honest with yourself and others, expressing yourself freely, and then taking responsibility for your choices.

Cultivate positive relationships. Being authentic means you are open and honest with your family, friends, and close associates. You build trust and intimacy by sharing your feelings, listening, and being supportive of others. Seek relationships with people who share your values. It can be challenging to conform to your values in an environment where others do not have the same standards.

*"Authenticity is a collection of choices
that we have to make every day.
It's about the choice to show up and be real.
The choice to be honest.
The choice to let our true selves be seen."*
Brene Brown

AN ILLUSTRATION

When Maria was a teenager, she loved to sing. She dreamed of becoming a famous singer someday and she practiced every day in her room. But her parents had other plans for her. They wanted her to pursue a more stable and lucrative career, such as law or medicine. Maria wanted to please her parents, so she did what they asked. She stopped singing and focused on her academics.

She got into a top law school and graduated with honors. She had everything that her parents wanted for her: a successful career, a big income, and a respectable reputation. But she was not happy. She felt empty and unfulfilled. So, one day she quit her job and enrolled in a music school. She started singing again and joined a band.

She had to deal with her parents and work very hard to improve her skills and find opportunities in the music industry. The end of the story was very positive for Maria. But it took a lot of work and courage.

Being authentic means we are true to ourselves, our values, and our dreams. Being authentic is rewarding, but it can also be hard. We should not ignore the advice or warnings of people who have our best interest in mind but we must decide who we are.[1]

"Accept no one's definition of your life: define yourself."
Anonymous

CHALLENGES

Being authentic is not always easy. It's important to be patient and resilient when the going gets difficult. Challenges you may encounter along the way might include:

Apathy

If you are generally content with your present circumstances you may resist changing or taking any risk. You may just choose to avoid new experiences or opportunities. You can end up limiting your potential by staying with what is familiar and comfortable.

Too transparent

Being authentic does not necessarily mean totally revealing yourself to others. You need to know your audience. Over-sharing can be unprofessional or inappropriate.

Feeling inferior

Being authentic may mean being vulnerable. It will be helpful if you understand your weaknesses and emotions. Authenticity can make you feel insecure or inadequate, especially if you compare yourself to others who seem more comfortable in their lives.

These challenges can be overcome by perseverance and patience. You may want to seek feedback from friends who will support you.

PRACTICAL APPLICATIONS

Authenticity can be challenging in a society that values conformity and perfection. Here are some tips for being more authentic:

1. *Accept your flaws, quirks, or weaknesses.*
Don't compare yourself to others. Embrace your uniqueness and utilize your strengths in pursuing your goals. Not everyone is an athlete. Some of us have trouble at math. Few of us are engineers. The point here is to know what you are *not* and to focus on building on your strengths, not risking your reputation on weaknesses.

2. *Stand firm on your beliefs and values.*
Don't compromise your honesty or integrity and don't abandon your

principles for the sake of popularity, convenience, or conformity. Stand firm on your principles and be honest with yourself and others.

3. *Know your achievements and contributions.*
Don't allow others to define your values or dictate your life. Be confident in who you are and be proud of your achievements.

4. *Analyze all important decisions.*
If it will impact your well-being or conflict with your core values it is important. Don't act impulsively out of fear or from peer pressure. Determine what aligns with your personal core values.

5. *Have a plan.*
Set goals, objectives, and life priorities that are consistent with your life purpose and core values. Don't let others determine your life.

6. *Practice authenticity.*
Take small actions that will allow you to establish who you are and what you value. Don't compromise your standards or pretend to be like others. Express your honest thoughts, feelings, and opinions.

7. *Seven simple tips:*
- Speak truthfully and avoid exaggerations.
- Stay true to your beliefs, values, and opinions.
- Express your passions without reservation.
- Be consistent. Align your actions with your words and values.
- When using social media be yourself – no false personas.
- Be willing to share your personal story.
- Be humble and approachable; don't be aloof.

> *"Authenticity is more than speaking; Authenticity is also about doing. Every decision we make says something about who we are."*
> Simon Sinek

IMPORTANCE TO AN EMPLOYER

Authenticity in the workplace means being yourself at work, being transparent with coworkers, and not putting on a persona for others.

Authenticity in the workplace will create increased employee engagement and more sincere relationships.

Being authentic will help employees develop strong relationships with their co-workers and bosses. This leads to greater job satisfaction, loyalty, and a desire to support the plans of the employer. It fosters a genuine and transparent work environment which helps produce open communication among team members.

Authenticity contributes to stronger leadership qualities. Employees who are true to themselves are more likely to lead with integrity, earning the respect and loyalty of their subordinates. Authentic leaders tend to be confident in their abilities, making them more adaptable and resilient in the face of work challenges.

In terms of relationships with customers, authenticity builds trust and credibility. When employees demonstrate sincerity and honesty, clients are more likely to form lasting connections with the company.

Overall, an employee who embraces authenticity not only contributes to a healthier work environment but enhances the organization's reputation. Their genuine approach to work makes them an invaluable asset to any employer.[0]

EXAMPLES: Authenticity Core Value Statements

1. I value living an authentic life, being sincere in every situation.

2. I will be true to myself. I will not be someone I'm not.

3. Authenticity will guide my decisions. I am true to my values.

4. I will honor my unique perspective and personal contributions.

5. I desire meaningful connections with people, fostering trust and mutual understanding.

6. Embracing vulnerability is a practice that allows me to grow and connect on a deeper level.

7. I prioritize being genuine over seeking external validation by conforming to other's values.

8. I choose to be authentic, communicating with truth, integrity, and respect in all situations.

9. I will be authentic in order to build a positive and supportive community around me.

MY PERSONAL CORE VALUE – Authenticity

Adopt or confirm your core value. If authenticity is already a core value, or if you want to establish it as a core value, write your personal core value in the space below. You may want to use the examples above as guides to draft your Personal Core Value Statement. Make it short, succinct, and meaningful to you. Something you can remember.

Authenticity:

_____

_____

_____

_____

_____

_____

THOUGHT AND DISCUSSION QUESTIONS

1. What does authenticity mean to you personally, and how do you see it influencing your thoughts and actions?

2. Can you think of an experience when you felt the impact of being authentic, either in your own actions or in someone else's? How did it affect the outcome of the situation?

3. How do you think embracing authenticity can enhance your relationships with others, both personally and professionally?

4. Can you recall an instance where authenticity played a significant role in forming a deeper connection with someone?

5. When have you felt truly authentic and genuine. What were the circumstances and how did it make you feel? Why?

6. What aspects of your life do you feel are not aligned with your true self? What would you need to do to change that?

7. How could embracing your personal authenticity lead to a more fulfilling life?

8. What fears or insecurities are holding you back? How could you overcome them?

9. How do you differentiate being authentic and being selfish? What boundaries do you believe are important to maintain?

10. What core values do you compromise when you're not being authentic? How could you align your actions with your beliefs?

"We are constantly invited to be who we are."
Henry David Thoreau

NOTES

I want to do the following:

a. _____
b. _____
c. _____
d. _____

I want to remember:

a. _____
b. _____
c. _____
d. _____

Action Challenge: Reflect on a situation where you felt pressured to conform to others' expectations. How did it make you feel? Identify one small way you can honor your true self in the coming week, even if it means going against the grain.

Chapter 7
Gratitude

GRATITUDE LIFE PRINCIPLE:
I will be thankful.

"Be thankful for what you have; you'll end up having more.
If you concentrate on what you don't have,
you will never, ever have enough."
Oprah Winfrey

GENERAL

Gratitude is a decision. You *decide* that you want to be thankful. You live with an appreciative attitude, whether or not you are satisfied or unhappy with your circumstances. This attitude is not necessarily something you learn or develop over time, rather it is more in the nature of a decision you make about life.

If you believe that life owes you success, happiness, and well-being, then you will tend to be dissatisfied with your life and circumstances. Alternatively you can decide you will be content whatever your situation. You can be grateful for whatever you have or whatever your circumstances. Life could be far worse!

This character trait is often established by the nature of your up-bringing and the attitudes of parents and family members. It is determined by what you value in life. If you are one who craves riches and if you don't have much, you tend to have a negative outlook toward life. You may find it difficult to be grateful for your life situation and what you do have.

However, if you are one who values relationships above material goods, your outlook on the value of things will tend to be determined by the joy of friends rather than the accumulation of wealth. Your attitudes can also be greatly influenced by the presence or absence of faith. Your outlook about your eternal future can have a significant impact on what is meaningful and important to you.

Gratitude is often associated with what makes you feel content or satisfied in your life. That contentment can be greatly impacted by your family and life circumstances. That's why gratitude is an attitude or a state of mind. You determine what is important to you and that will determine your level of thankfulness.

Gratitude does not mean one accepts the lack of things that would make life better or easier. You may be working very hard to make life better. Working hard to have a better life in the future does not mean you cannot be thankful for what you have today. I may wish for better circumstances, but I will not live my life anchored to the lack of things over which I have very little control.

> *"We should certainly count our blessings,*
> *but we should also make our blessings count."*
> Neal A. Maxwell

Definition

By definition gratitude is a feeling or emotion of being thankful and appreciative for what you have. It is a positive response to another's kindness, generosity, or help. It has the inherent characteristic of recognizing value and goodness. Gratitude comes from a Latin word meaning "pleasing" or "thankful." It can be expressed by words or actions that demonstrate kindness, warmth, or generosity. Its focus is on the positive aspects of your life. Real gratitude often produces action. We can use what we have to help produce something better for ourselves, our family, or for others.

Having an attitude of gratitude does not mean we are content with bad life situations. Thankfulness means you are grateful for the good things in your life. And it certainly doesn't mean you should not try to improve bad circumstances.

The point in Neal Maxwell's quote above is that we use the good or positive things we have and make them useful in our life. In other words we should not allow the lack of something desirable to prevent us from using something positive in our life.

This can be illustrated by someone who is disabled. It might be very easy to allow that disability to prevent one from doing anything but sitting at home fretting about or blaming the circumstances of life. Experience has illustrated that those disabled people who use their other abilities, no matter how small, to make themselves useful can be valuable contributors to society. Some have even said they were grateful for their disability. That can be hard to understand and I think you have to live it to really understand, but that demonstrates why gratitude is a decision and not a feeling or emotion.

There are three important aspects of gratitude. First, it is the attitude of being thankful for the good things of life. Second, it is the gratitude for what you have and not complaining about what you don't have. Lastly, it is the practice of expressing that gratitude to others.

> *"Gratitude is a quality similar to electricity:*
> *it must be produced and discharged*
> *and used up in order to exist at all."*
> William Faulkner

PRACTICING GRATITUDE

People who actively practice being thankful in their circumstances have real feelings of peace and contentment. We do not have to feel deprived simply because we cannot buy a new car, go on an expensive vacation, or take our family to a theme park. Rather we are thankful we have a car that operates, we can take day trips to local parks to get away from the day-to-day drudgery, and periodically enjoy family time at a great national or state park.

Compare the happiness of eating an expensive steak to a good fast food dinner. How long does the happiness last? Not very long and it all ends up in the same place! So what is the additional value of the few hours when life was lived at a much higher level of satisfaction? I would suggest that if your dinner companions were good friends and your conversation stimulating, the difference is relatively minor.

The point here is that the expense of the meal and the nature of the surroundings may have some impact on the experience. But the conversation and the sharing that took place during the meal is what will be remembered and not the taste of the food or ambiance of the expensive meal.

Decide to feel privileged and be grateful for your opportunity to be with people you enjoy. Don't feel short-changed because you are not able to dine at five star restaurants or hob-nob with people who think they are important.

Eckhart Tolle has said, "Acknowledging the good that you already have in your life is the foundation for all abundance." Regardless of who we are or the nature of our life situation, there is something (often much) to be grateful for in our lives. Whatever that is, invest your time and thought in uplifting and positive things.

Gratitude is a great character trait for generating joy, satisfaction, and contentment. It requires investing in life regardless of your social standing, financial condition, or health status. Make a decision to be grateful and thankful.

But there are times when being thankful can be difficult. For example:

- When we are *experiencing* difficult times.
- When we are *surrounded* by overwhelming negativity.
- When we *feel* that we have nothing to be grateful for.
- When there is no hope.

> **"He is a wise man who does not grieve for the things**
> **which he has not, but rejoices for those which he has."**
> Epictetus

THANKFULNESS SHOULD BE EVIDENT

You decide to be satisfied. You decide to be generous. Your gratitude is evident in the way you live. You can say a number of things about your circumstances but if your actions don't demonstrate gratitude, your gratitude is probably only skin deep.

Someone who is truly thankful for what he has will share that with others. It might be material things or it could be simple kindness because one cares about others. Your generosity might be "time" because you are blessed with the ability to fix things. Generosity does not necessarily mean money. Sharing your excess, whether it is money, compassion, or skill, will produce great personal satisfaction.

Positive attitudes and thankfulness for your own situation can be contagious in the lives of others. If you demonstrate the ability to share simple kindnesses, you and those you impact will be blessed. If you demonstrate joy and pleasure in your gratitude, your attitude will be evident to those around you.

I know someone who is always humming. I understand it sometimes drives his spouse crazy, but he has a positive and friendly demeanor and he is always humming to himself. It's pretty hard to think he lets the vagaries of life dictate his attitude.

> *"Silent gratitude isn't very much to anyone."*
> Gertrude Stein

BE GRATEFUL FOR OTHERS

Great joy and satisfaction can be gained from relationships and particularly family members and good friends. If you have ever had a true best friend you know how valuable they are. Even casual friends are valuable to our well-being. They all add much to our life.

In some case they might perform tasks for us that we cannot do easily ourselves. They can give us advice about matters we know little about. They are often sounding boards who can help relieve stress and anxiety. Many times they can simply provide their presence. Being there means we are not alone which is often a meaningful gift. We should always be thankful for those around us who are supportive of our needs or wants.

The following quote from Ralph Marston expresses a valuable truth. Be thankful to those around you. Say thank you. Show appreciation even for minor things. Do you thank your server at the local café? Do you thank the check-out clerks at the grocery store or the person bagging your items? Make it a habit to thank those around you for their service, whether you are paying for it or not.

DO IT IN ALL TIMES AND CIRCUMSTANCES

Your gratitude should be evident in both public and private situations. It should occur for both big and little things. Thankfulness should be evident for the normal daily activities like shopping, not just for lavish gestures. It should be evident for both the basics and the extravagant. Why? Because it is evidence of your attitude! It is an expression of your inner feeling of gratefulness whether it is for a mundane obligation or someone going the extra mile.

Gratitude should saturate your life. For example:
- For a celebration of birth or for a life well-lived.
- For the opportunity to plant and for the privilege to harvest.
- For a time to cry and for a time to laugh.
- For a time to grieve and for a time to celebrate.
- For a time to travel and a time to settle down.
- For a time to embrace life and for a time to pull back.
- For a time to search and a time to celebrate the found.
- For a time to cherish and a time to throw away.
- For a time to tear down and a time to fix.
- For a time to be quiet and a time to speak.

There are many different times and seasons in our life and we can be grateful for each experience or we can be discontent. It is a choice we make in how we want to live our life. We can be thankful we are alive or we can be ungrateful because life is sometimes difficult.
Make no mistake, we choose how we engage in the game of life. It all depends how you choose to think about it.

> *"The soul that gives thanks can find comfort in everything;*
> *the soul that complains can find comfort in nothing."*
> Hannah Whitall Smith

For everything

Some would suggest that we should be grateful in everything and for all circumstances. Being grateful for everything seems a bit over the top. It's easy to understand why one would be grateful for wisdom, understanding, wealth, or power. Living an abundant life would certainly be attractive and something to be desired but why or how could anyone be grateful for scarcity? How would it be possible for one to be grateful for times of suffering or lack of basic necessities?

Being grateful for everything good, bad, boring, frustrating, exciting, tremendous, or tragic does not seem possible. We might be able to understand someone suggesting not to worry or be anxious, but being thankful for difficult times makes no sense.

I cannot fully explain the suggestion of being thankful in everything. But I believe the answer lies in separating the reality and the mindset. I do not think the idea or concept of being grateful for everything means we necessarily appreciate physical suffering. Nobody (or very few people) could find a reason to be thankful for experiencing serious health problems or painful physical loss.

Rather, I think the point is that in the general course of life we hold to a positive attitude and *decide* that we will not allow the negative experiences in life to destroy our spirit or dictate how we respond to the challenges in life. I am certainly not going to celebrate losing a leg in an accident, but I am not going to allow that reality to dictate how I face life without a leg. I will choose to be grateful that I did not lose both legs or did not suffer other disabilities. I will choose to face life with a positive attitude because I will not allow the disability to destroy my life or my spirit.

But there is always someone who will say, "Does this mean that when my house burns down, I am thankful for my house being destroyed?" This is the example of looking at the glass as half full or half empty. What do you want to focus on in a bad situation: the loss or what was not lost? The positive individual is going to be grateful no one was injured and that the house ultimately can be replaced. The devastated person will focus on the loss of things, most of which can be replaced.

How should we deal with loss? What do you do when you are faced with disaster? How do you deal with living during times of suffering and high stress? First, you cannot go back in time and prevent the circumstances. You could ask the question what you might learn from the tragedy. You might consider how your life could be positively impacted because of the situation. Is there something you can learn from the circumstance, no matter how terrible the loss? Is there some positive result that could occur because of this experience? These questions will take time to process and the answers may not be obvious, but keep them in the forefront of your thoughts as you struggle through the months and even years that follow.

"If you want to find happiness, find gratitude."
Steve Maraboli

FOCUS ON THE IMPORTANT THINGS

Be thankful for internal peace, hope, and joy that you experience every day. Don't worry about tomorrow. Let tomorrow take care of itself. Each day has enough trouble or challenges of its own. Nothing can be gained by worrying about what tomorrow may bring.

Focus on the good things in your life. What brings you happiness and joy? What gives you hope? Seek good things that will build you up or establish a solid foundation in your life. Obviously you cannot ignore troubles but you don't have to dwell on them. Deal with the difficulties in life and then put them behind you.

Seek those things that bring joy, satisfaction, and contentment in the future. Don't live in the past. Those things that are right and good will provide lasting satisfaction. Joy is produced when you have that inner feeling of delight or gladness. It can be a moderate feeling of satisfaction or a high degree of exultation. Regardless of the level of emotion that may accompany your joy, there is an underlying feeling of contentment and understanding that you are right with the world.

These feelings can be about present circumstances, future hope, or eternal well-being. The feeling that takes permanent residence in your heart is often evidenced by gratitude, cheerfulness, and a sense that life will be good no matter the circumstances.

We know that if our focus is on love, patience, kindness, goodness, faithfulness, gentleness, trust, and self-control, those characteristics will produce joy, peace, and contentment. Joy can also arise out of the performance of doing good things. Good works produce a peace and serenity which will allow one to be grateful for life, friends, and even the daily grind.

"Strive to find things to be thankful for,
and just look for the good in who you are."
Bethany Hamilton

PRACTICAL TIPS

Demonstrating gratitude doesn't have to be complicated. Here are some simple and easy tips to practice gratitude in your daily life:

1. Thank someone to show gratitude:
   a. Spouse: Give him/her a hug.
   b. Children: Give child a special dinner plate.
   c. Parents: Help with housework or errands.
   d. Friend: Babysit.
   e. Pastor: Note of appreciation or support.
   f. Employer: Do the very best work you can do.

2. Write down three things you are grateful for each day.

3. Write notes to show appreciation for acts of kindness.

4. Make a habit to remind yourself of the good things in life.

5. Appreciate the simple pleasures.

6. Offer genuine compliments to others to recognize their effort.

7. Say "Thank-you" whenever you receive something.

8. Take time to appreciate the beauty of nature around you.

9. Before going to sleep, think of one thing you were grateful for.

10. Practice gratitude with a friend. Describe why you are grateful.

11. Practice random acts of kindness.

12. Institute new morning or evening routines.
    - read a quote each morning about being grateful,
    - before going to work say out loud what you're grateful for,

He who does not give thanks for little, will not be thankful for much!

IMPORTANCE TO AN EMPLOYER

An employer will highly value an employee who embodies gratitude. It goes beyond mere politeness, fostering a positive workplace culture that can significantly impact productivity, employee satisfaction, and overall company success.

Grateful employees are more likely to be motivated and engaged in their work. When individuals recognize and appreciate the opportunities provided by the company, they feel a sense of loyalty and commitment. This heightened engagement translates into increased productivity and a willingness to go the extra mile for the organization or its customers.

Grateful employees tend to be more resilient in the face of challenges. They focus on solutions rather than dwelling on problems. Their optimistic outlook can inspire their colleagues during difficult times.

Grateful employees are likely to exhibit greater interpersonal skills. They acknowledge the efforts of their colleagues and express appreciation for their contributions. This creates a supportive atmosphere which builds strong relationships among team members and promotes more effective communication and teamwork.

Employees with gratitude as a core value are less likely to succumb to entitlement or negative behaviors. Instead, they are generally more humble and appreciative of constructive feedback.

From an employer's perspective, a workforce that embodies gratitude can lead to higher employee retention rates. When employees feel valued and appreciated by a grateful employer, they are less likely to seek opportunities elsewhere, reducing turnover and the associated costs of hiring and training new staff.[0]

EXAMPLES: Gratitude Core Value Statements

1. I believe in cultivating a grateful mindset, appreciating the blessings and kindness I receive daily.

2. I embrace thankfulness as a guiding principle, expressing gratitude for both big and small moments in life.

3. I value the power of appreciation, recognizing the efforts and contributions of others with genuine thanks.

4. I embody graciousness, extending gratitude to those who touch my life with kindness and compassion.

5. I approach life with humble gratitude, recognizing that everything I have is a gift to be cherished.

6. I prioritize embracing the blessings in my life, fostering a sense of appreciation and gratitude.

7. My core value is daily gratitude, taking time each day to reflect on the positive aspects of my life.

8. I will nurture a grateful spirit that radiates appreciation and spreads positivity to those around me.

9. I demonstrate gratitude through my actions, treating others with kindness and respect.

10. I embrace gratitude as a way of life, enriching my existence and influencing others to do the same.

MY PERSONAL CORE VALUE – Gratitude

Adopt or confirm your core value. If gratitude is already a core value, or if you want to establish it as a core value, write your personal core value in the space below. You may want to use the examples above as guides to draft your Personal Core Value Statement. Make it short, succinct, and meaningful to you. Something you can easily remember.

Gratitude:

_____
_____
_____
_____
_____
_____
_____
_____

DISCUSSION AND THOUGHT QUESTIONS

1. What is the source of your personal joy? What are you deeply thankful to for?

2. What are you thankful for in others? Why?

3. How do you presently demonstrate a thankful attitude?

4. What is your typical body language?
   a. Do you ever sing quietly to yourself, hum, or smile?
   b. Do you walk with a lively step?
   c. What are you looking at?

5. Do you think it is really possible to have an attitude of gratitude in tragic circumstances or when life is difficult?

6. How has expressing gratitude positively impacted your life or the lives of others around you?

7. Think of a time when you received genuine appreciation. How did it make you feel? How did it influence your relationships?

8. What challenges might prevent people from expressing gratitude regularly? How can they be overcome?

9. How do you think cultivating gratitude helps us develop a more positive outlook on life?

10. Reflect on a time when you may have overlooked expressing gratitude to someone who deserved it. What did you learn from that experience?

11. How does gratitude foster a sense of interconnectedness and strengthen social bonds in personal and professional relationships?

12. Explore the connection between gratitude and resilience. How can a grateful mindset help us bounce back from challenges and setbacks?

"If a fellow isn't thankful for what he's got,
he isn't likely to be thankful for
what he's going to get."
Frank A. Clark

NOTES

<u>I want to do the following:</u>

a. _____
b. _____
c. _____
d. _____

<u>I want to remember:</u>

a. _____
b. _____
c. _____
d. _____

Action Challenge: Start a gratitude journal and commit to writing down three things you're grateful for each day. At the end of the week, reflect on how this practice has shifted your perspective and enhanced your overall well-being.

Chapter 8
Generosity

GENEROSITY LIFE PRINCIPLE:
I will be generous.

*"You have not lived until you
have done something for someone
who can never repay you."*
John Bunyan

GENERAL

Webster's Dictionary says that being generous is giving liberally. Being generous can also be described as being magnanimous, charitable, or open-handed.

The opposite of being generous is often described as being cheap, close-fisted, or even miserly. More serious words might include greed, avarice, and covetous.

Many years ago a stranger gave my friend's grandmother (age 20 at the time) a penny to ride the bus home. A penny doesn't sound like much but the bus ride cost 20 cents and she had only 19! In this case a penny was the difference between a ride home or a long walk! This grandmother was still telling the story about the generous person when she was in her nineties. Why? Because it made a lasting impression and it meant a great deal to her at the time. Anonymous givers often have little knowledge about the impact their gifts have on the recipients of their generosity. Has someone else's generosity ever impacted you in some way? Is generosity something you think about? Are you generous? Do you want to be?

Generosity is usually thought about in terms of money. It is often the giving of something of monetary value, but it can also be simply the giving or doing something beyond that which was required or expected. It can be sharing something you have with another. It might be generosity of time or expertise. It might be doing something for someone in need.

The subject of generosity always reminds me of the story about the beggar who asked a stranger for money. The stranger dug out his billfold and handed the beggar a dollar. When the stranger did this he said, "I'll give you money – not because you deserve it but because it pleases me." "Thank you, sir," the beggar replied, "but while you're at it, why don't you make it a ten and thoroughly enjoy yourself!"

> *"Real generosity is doing something nice*
> *for someone who will never find out."*
> Frank A. Clark

Types of generosity

There are several different aspects or categories of generosity:

Giving: Generosity is the giving of time, money, resources, expertise, or possessions to someone.

Volunteering: Volunteering is a form of generosity that specifically involves giving time or expertise to help others.

Charity: Charity is a form of generosity that usually involves giving money or goods to help others, particularly those in need.

Sharing: Sharing is a form of generosity that involves giving or loaning your possessions to another.

Influence: This involves applying influence to matters for the benefit of others. This might take the form of words, physical support, or written or verbal endorsement.

Kindness: Many acts of kindness are the result of a generous heart. They are acts that make a positive difference in someone's life.

> *"Because that's what kindness is. It's not doing*
> *something for someone else because they can't,*
> *but because you can."*
> Andrew Iskander

MONEY RULES

Life is not defined by what we have. The world will easily lead you to the conclusion that happiness and joy is a result of the amount and value of your possessions. How important is money and wealth? What are you willing to do to acquire and protect your wealth? What does your income, money, or wealth determine in your life? It may determine a lot more than you might first think. It will:

- determine where you live,
- define the size and quality of your home,
- determine the quality of the clothes you can buy,
- determine both the quantity and quality of the food you eat,
- often restrict the education you can acquire,
- determine your lifestyle,
- limit the type of entertainment you can enjoy,
- restrict the type and value of your healthcare, and
- influence the friends you can acquire.

Consider then what your income, money, or wealth does <u>not</u> determine in your life. It will generally not define your character, but it might have a big impact. It should not determine what you believe about truth, but it can have influence. It should not impact whether you have a faith, but your self-reliance and success can cause you to think you can do anything you want, and therefore faith is meaningless. Wealth can cause one to become very self-reliant.

It seems obvious that the world and its values, particularly money and wealth, have a bigger impact on life issues than you might first imagine!

THE BIG DANGER: Greed

Greed is the desire to have more of something than you need. Someone who has a billion dollars doesn't need more money but if they are driven by a very strong desire to have more, that becomes greed. That excessive desire or drive (greed) can consume one's thoughts and actions and drive one to make decisions, based not on good/bad or right/wrong, but simply on the desire to gain more.

Greedy people are likely to:

- oppress or ignore the poor in order to enrich themselves,
- be driven to gain more wealth,
- provoke conflict among friends and associates in order to accomplish financial goals,
- be penalized or reprimanded for their behavior, and
- be ignored when they are in real need of help.

The need to accumulate wealth will often result in cutting corners, cheating, lying, and making choices based on gaining more wealth. The greedy person is likely to provoke conflict because their primary interest is in accumulating more for themselves.

Greedy people have different lifestyle objectives which will result in behavior that can be obnoxious, self-centered, high risk, and sometimes without concern for others. They often practice deceit and use devious methods to fulfill their desire to gain more wealth.

People suffering from greed will ignore the poor, needy, and disadvantaged. Society expects those who have excess to share with those who do not. Greed simply violates what most people consider worthy personal character. People who hold self in such high esteem generous behavior is prevented are often the butt of jokes and are frequently ignored if they ever need help themselves.

ANXIETY AND WORRY

Wealthy people often harbor the concern that someone might try to steal what they have acquired. Thus, money, time, and effort must be invested to protect what has been accumulated. Anxiety can cause sleepless nights for someone trying to guard his wealth.

Worry and anxiety also occur because the greedy person is never satisfied with what they have. Because they never have enough, they are constantly worried about the future. Thus, they are continually searching for ways to gain more. Stress is the natural result of the anxiety surrounding maintaining wealth. Such a lifestyle is futile and a never-ending cycle of unfulfilled desire, worry, and dissatisfaction.

Have you ever wanted something badly and then when you got it, you craved more? It might be money, a rich dessert, a new car, a new house, a better job. How did this craving impact your life? When you achieved the desired result, what happened? Were you satisfied? The craving for more and protecting what you have produces anxiety.

The inherent problem with wealth is that it has no eternal value. You can't take it with you. Wealth does not automatically bring joy. It can certainly bring temporary happiness, but it also brings a whole new set of problems and responsibilities.

Wealth usually does not produce better or more worthwhile relationships. Wealth is more likely to destroy friendships. Why? Because the focus is on money, wealth, and power, and not on caring, spending time together, and developing relationships.

Wealth and possessions must be managed, and managed well. The management alone can be taxing. It can be a full time job! All of that can be stressful.

GENEROSITY PRODUCES REWARDS

Many people believe that those who give freely will be rewarded for their good behavior. They also believe that if they are selfish they are likely to suffer loss. There is the general concept expressed in many proverbs that the generous person will be enriched and the greedy person cursed.

The generous person generally does what is expected – something that is morally, legally, or ethically right. The selfish person may refuse to do what is right. This is obviously not always true, but it is a general rule. Generally, generosity is rewarded and good things happen to good people. If you sow goodness you will reap goodness. If you sow dishonesty, then you are most likely to be treated in the same way.

You may have heard it said that everybody loves the rich! Why? I suspect because there is the hope of being blessed by their power and wealth. You may expect a piece of the action if you are close to the seat of power and wealth. But it is also said that whoever shows kindness to the poor will be happy. Can both concepts be true?

On the other hand, someone who is generous to the poor is generally not looking to receive some monetary gain in return. Acts of kindness and generosity cause you to be content and filled with some measure of joy because you were able to help and even relieve the suffering of another. It is the pure act of generosity that produces this feeling, not the hope of a reward.

Let's be clear at this point: we are talking about real kindness and generosity. We are not talking about the person who speaks kind words but does nothing. What good are nice words to someone who is cold, hungry, or without shelter? Talk is useless for the needy and disadvantaged who are suffering. To recognize true need and ignore it reflects an uncaring and even evil spirit.

> *"Giving frees us from the familiar territory*
> *of our own needs by opening our mind to the*
> *unexplained worlds occupied*
> *by the needs of others."*
> Barbara Bush

WEALTH IS A RESPONSIBILITY

Many believe that the wealthy have a responsibility to help the needy. The disadvantaged frequently have no voice and their need is often hidden by the noise of the world. The help we provide should not be for show or the benefit of those watching but to meet the real need of those suffering.

We all have a responsibility to defend the cause of the needy and be true to our core values. It may be in the form of giving money. It may mean we give time and help to a food pantry or shelter. It may mean we help the homeless or help build a home with Habitat For Humanity. Maybe we are a mentor, tutor, or Big Brother. Maybe we serve in a nursing home. Maybe we give money to help children in the social service system. Regardless of what it is, we do <u>something</u>.

> *Generosity is a heart condition.*
> *Protect your heart!*

CHALLENGES

The challenges of being generous can sometimes be overwhelming if it is not a core value that comes naturally to you. It can be particularly

111

difficult if it is not something that was common in your household when you were growing up. If that is your situation it just takes some time and practice. Yes, practice! It's much easier the second time.

It can also be difficult to be generous when you are personally struggling financially. If money is tight for you and you feel drawn to be generous, give your time, expertise, or skills. Generosity is not just giving money, although that's often the first thing we think about. Generosity is a state of mind that looks for ways to be kind and caring to someone. Who do you know that needs a helping hand?

It can be difficult to be generous when you are not really sure how to help. This may require a little more intentionality. What are your interests? What impacts your heart? Do you have friends who are generous or compassionate? What are they doing? Find a friend who wants to be generous and undertake the journey together.

DEVELOPING GENEROSITY

There must be a little "want to" in your make-up. If there is no desire to be generous it can be difficult to start helping others. If there is no inner urging to be generous or you are not sure where to start, you may want to consider the following:

- Make a list of what interests you; skills that could be shared, and special knowledge you possess.

- What are you passionate about? Is it animals, nature, people, housing, the homeless, etc.?

- Think about your list and consider how you could use your assets to help someone in need.

- Start small. There is no need to jump in with both feet. You can sign up for newsletters from charities or ministries that are involved with things that interest you.

- Recruit someone to join you in the process of discovery. Ask someone in your family, a close friend, or co-worker.

It is really not as hard as you may think. If you get involved with something that is not working for you, find something else that does work. Ask friends, family, bosses, and mentors for advice.

BENEFITS OF GENEROSITY

There are a number of real personal benefits for being generous. You may not experience all of these benefits but most of them will occur over time when you are truly generous.

1. *Health:* Generosity will result in a more healthy life! Many studies confirm this. Being generous will make you feel better mentally and emotionally. It can even fight depression leading to increased joy, contentment, satisfaction, and hope.

2. *Stress*: It will reduce stress because it takes the focus off yourself.

3. *Purpose*: It will give you a sense of purpose.

4. *Community*: It will introduce you to other generous people. There is a common sense of community among those who come together to help others. It can help you connect with others and build stronger relationships.

5. *Identity:* It will raise your self-esteem.

Generous people are often blessed! There are many positive aspects to being generous and many personal rewards. Speak up for those who have no voice. The poor, needy, and disadvantaged of the world will always be with us. The value of our lives may be judged by how we treat those in need!

TIPS FOR BEING GENEROUS

Being generous is not hard work. It can be relatively easy. Some examples you might want to consider are:

1. Helping a friend move into a new apartment or offering them a place to stay if they need it.

2. Paying for the coffee of the person in line behind you or buying a meal for a homeless person.

3. Offering advice to a student hoping to break into your industry or mentoring someone who wants to learn from you.

4. Paying vet fees to neuter your neighborhood's stray cats or dogs. Or adopt an animal from a shelter.

5. Tipping your restaurant server more than the standard amount or leaving a positive review for their service.

6. Volunteering at a soup kitchen or donating food, clothes, or money to a charity.

7. Lending your car to someone who needs it to get to their job.

8. Going to your local retirement home and reading and talking to senior citizens. Or send cards or flowers.

9. Giving money to your local food bank to purchase food.

10. Giving money to a needy student to help fund their education.

When we are generous, we are not only helping others, but we are also making the world a better place. Part of the difficulty today in the Western world is that we live in an environment of excess. We have far more than we need. We could give away much of what we have and our lives would not be impacted. We have much that we never use. How much of your "stuff," your money, or your time, could you give to others because you don't really need it? Maybe a lot!

> *"There never was any heart truly great and generous*
> *that was not also tender and compassionate."*
> Robert Frost

FINAL WORD

There are many people who save what they have so they can give it away. They are not driven by the need to have the best things in life, but rather how their lives can provide a better life for others. Some are so driven that they are constantly putting the needs of others ahead of their own. They receive great satisfaction in helping the disadvantaged and not accumulating more for themselves. This does not mean they live in want but the value of their lives is based on how well they serve others rather than themselves. They do not believe that life is defined by the amount or quality of their possessions.

How do you want to be remembered? Do you want your tombstone to read that you died a rich man or that, "He had many friends because he cared." What is important to you? What is your core value regarding being generous? How do you want to be remembered?

IMPORTANCE TO AN EMPLOYER

An employer would highly value an employee who holds generosity as a personal core value because it exhibits a selfless and compassionate nature which would foster a positive and harmonious work environment. The willingness to help others without expecting anything in return cultivates a sense of support among team members, leading to increased cooperation and productivity.

A generous employee is often an excellent collaborator and team player. He is more likely to share knowledge, offer assistance, and support his colleagues. This contributes to the overall growth and success of the organization.

Generous employees tend to excel in customer relations. The genuine concern for others and willingness to go the extra mile creates a positive and memorable experience for clients. This boosts customer loyalty and enhances the company's reputation.

Overall, an employee who values generosity brings many positive attributes to the workplace. Employers recognize the profound impact such individuals can have on organizational culture and success, making them highly sought after and valued members of any team.[0]

EXAMPLES: Generosity Core Value Statements

Following are sample core value statements for someone who wants to adopt generosity as a personal core value:

1. I value generosity as a guiding principle in all aspects of my life, seeking opportunities to help and support others.

2. I believe in the transformative impact of generosity.

3. Generosity will shape my actions and decisions, driving me to make a difference in the lives of others.

4. I embrace a lifestyle of giving, caring, and compassion, striving to be generous with my time, money, and resources.

5. I prioritize generosity as a way to build stronger connections and foster a more caring and inclusive environment.

6. I will be generous in order to share my excess with others.

7. I will be generous to those in need, exhibiting empathy and goodwill to the disadvantaged.

8. I embrace the core value of generosity and selflessness in order to make a difference in people's lives.

9. Generosity will be a driving force in my life.

10. My life's purpose is to embody generosity in all interactions, enriching the lives I encounter with kindness and care.

MY PERSONAL CORE VALUE – Generosity

Adopt or confirm your core value. If generosity is already a core value, or if you want to establish it as a core value, write your personal core value statement in the space below. You may want to use the examples above as guides to draft your Personal Core Value Statement. Make it short, succinct, and meaningful to you. Something you can easily remember.

Generosity:

_____
_____
_____
_____
_____
_____
_____
_____

DISCUSSION AND THOUGHT QUESTIONS

1. What is your favorite story or experience about generosity?

2. Do you consider yourself generous? Why? Why not?

3. What does generosity mean to you on a personal level? How has it influenced your life, either as the giver or the recipient?

4. Share a specific instance in which someone's generous act had a profound impact on your life in some way? Explain.

5. In your opinion, how does practicing generosity benefit both the giver and the receiver? Can you think of examples?

6. Which one of the dangers of being greedy concerns you the most? Why?

7. Which one of the above "Benefits of Generosity" have you found or know to be true? Explain.

8. What do you consider to be the basic motivator for being generous? Explain.

9. Reflecting on times when you might have hesitated to be generous, what were the underlying reasons you held back? What could you have done differently to embrace a more generous approach?

10. Generosity is often associated with material or financial giving, but it has many forms. What do you think is the most important non-material act of generosity? Why?

11. If you were a generous person, but had no financial resources, what would you personally do to demonstrate and practice your generosity?

12. How can one person's generosity influence or encourage others to be generous? Do you have a real life example?

NOTES

<u>I want to do the following:</u>

a. _____
b. _____
c. _____
d. _____

<u>I want to remember:</u>

a. _____
b. _____
c. _____
d. _____

Action Challenge: Identify a way you can be generous with your time, resources, or kindness this week. It could be volunteering, donating to a cause you care about, or simply offering a helping hand to someone in need. Reflect on how this act of generosity impacts both you and the recipient.

Chapter 9
Kindness and Goodness

GOODNESS LIFE PRINCIPLE:
I will be good and kind to others.

"Do all the good you can,
By all the means you can,
In all the ways you can,
In all the places you can,
At all the times you can,
To all the people you can,
As long as ever you can."
John Wesley

GENERAL

Kindness and goodness are similar in nature but they actually have a different focus. It is useful to understand the precise definitions of these two terms.

> **KINDNESS:** having a desire to help others; trying to bring happiness to others; being helpful; the characteristic or attitude of showing sympathy; loving; considerate; and thoughtful.

> **GOODNESS:** morally good; doing what is right; favorable character; virtuous; commendable; benevolent; praiseworthy character; or beneficial. Synonyms for goodness include decent; moral; honest; integrity; righteous; and upright. (Merriam-Webster)

Being good also includes being ready to be kind, forgiving, grateful, righteous, humble, and most of the positive and uplifting character traits we discuss in this book. All people deserve to be treated with the same kindness with which you yourself would wish to be treated.

Kindness or goodness should not be a reaction to the treatment by others, but rather an intended response because it's the right or caring thing to do. If we are treated unkindly our response should not be to treat the offender with the same uncaring behavior. Because we all fail to act properly at times, our response should not be to return unkindness with more unkindness. There is nothing to be gained by continued poor behavior. The one offended should choose the high road, which may teach a valuable lesson to the offender.

"Goodness is the only investment that never fails."
Henry David Thoreau

GRACE

Grace generally refers to the practice of responding with class, dignity, or elegance when such a positive response is not deserved or warranted by the behavior of the offender. Another explanation of grace is that it is courteous goodwill.

Our response to unkindness should be grace. Assume that you are treated very badly for no reason. What do you think will be the response of the guilty party if you respond in kind? Alternatively, what is the observer's response if you react in a kind and loving manner? Generally the response by the guilty party is an immediate apology. A negative response is more likely to spark conflict and confrontation. Stop for a minute and think what the bystander is thinking about you in each of these two possible response scenarios.

Let's face it: we have all been unkind when we did not really intend to be hurtful. Our tongue simply spoke before our brains had the opportunity to think about what we were saying. It is easy to choose a bad response when we are having a bad day. Sometimes we are just tired. The person who sets us off has no idea we are hurting and their words are often overblown in our minds.

Rather than react emotionally, we should always be prepared to offer grace. We all deserve a measure of grace from time to time.

The fruit of grace is peace rather than stress or displeasure. We make a conscious effort to choose kindness over cruelty. Your life can exude light rather than darkness if you decide that is your goal.

Think how you would want to be treated and treat others in a like manner. We choose how we respond to the words and actions of others. It can be good or bad. As the saying goes, "You are likely to catch more with honey than you are with vinegar."

> *"If you hope for mercy, show mercy.*
> *If you look for kindness, show kindness."*
> Kerry Weber

GUARD YOUR SPEECH

One of the easier ways to create conflict is to say something that is offensive to someone or demonstrate a lack of respect for another person. When we act with pride and arrogance we are likely to insult and offend others. Nobody likes to be belittled. If we treat others with contempt, we are likely to be on the receiving end of retaliation because of our uncaring attitude.

Nothing good is ever gained from disrespect. Wounding the pride of others is a good way to lose friends quickly. Being offensive is not an attractive character trait. Patience and perseverance are more reasonable ways to deal with someone's poor behavior.

There are many wise sayings that suggest remaining silent at an offense can promote reconciliation. Quick tempers promote conflict. Offensive words will cause strife instead of resolution. There is no law that says we must respond in kind to bad behavior.

One might wonder why overlooking an offense is a better course of action than a snappy put-down. It can certainly be very difficult, particularly if one suffers because of the bad behavior. Obviously, not all offenses should be overlooked, but often, turning the other cheek is a wise choice. It takes two to make a fight and confrontation almost always is a poor choice.

Insults can produce broken hearts or despair. The party who has been verbally injured may try to overlook the hurt, but it can be devastating depending on the nature of the insult. Recipients of harsh words frequently need comfort and sympathy – not tough love. Their feelings and emotions can be seriously affected and they may be reluctant to face others if the insult is particularly embarrassing. In very serious situations they can feel isolated and hopeless. This can permanently impact the nature of relationships.

"Speaking kind words starts a wave of love
in motion that brings more love upon your shores."
Molly Friedenfeld

DON'T BE UNKIND

The kind person who exhibits a caring attitude toward others will cause similar beneficial conduct to be directed toward his needs. The unkind or cruel individual will create animosity and strife. You may know unkind people who have suffered because of the way they treat others. Poor behavior produces a bad reputation and an unkind person will eventually lose friends because of that behavior.

Kindness attracts like behavior, supporters, and friends. The easiest way to lose friends is to be unkind. Nobody wants to associate with unkind people.

Many proverbs and wise sayings focus on bad behavior. Some typical themes are:

- The good obtain favor and schemers are condemned.
- People do not forget those who return good for evil.
- It is unjust to penalize an honest person for his integrity.
- It is improper to show partiality in making judgments.
- The one leading others into evil ways may find disaster.

Very few people want to associate with those who exhibit the characteristics described above. Evil people and schemers have a difficult time living and working in a normal society. Their reputations alone prevent them from living a normal life.

In some cases the unkind behavior crosses the line to the immoral or illegal. Small offenses can grow into substantial evil. Then it is no longer an inconvenience but a substantial injustice.

"Be kind! Everyone you meet is fighting a harder battle."
Plato

ADVICE

Practice goodness and kindness continually in your life. You may be a light in a dark place that needs illumination. When it is in your power, your words and actions should be kind and healing, not damaging. Goodness should be your norm and your first response in all circumstances. It should be your natural and expected behavior, not the occasional occurrence.

When someone does you a kindness you should try to return that kindness at an opportune time. You cannot always control what happens, but you can demonstrate appropriate attitudes, speech, and action when they are in your control.

Ignore Insults

Fools will quickly tell you when they are not happy. They never seem to remain silent! Those who ignore insults deserve commendation because it is not easy to ignore fools. The best way to disarm the one with an unkind tongue is to act as if their words do not matter.

There is much to be gained by ignoring insults. Peace will be maintained, strife will be avoided, and there will be no visible wounds. Ignoring insults will take the air out of poor behavior.

Ignoring such behavior will also give time a chance to dissipate the situation. Wounds can often be more easily healed in private. A measured and caring response will go a long way in resolving a situation that could easily escalate to something worse.

If your natural response is to match insult with insult, somebody is very likely to go over the line and serious confrontation can result. People who are used to being sarcastic on social media can easily allow their behavior to spill over to rudeness in face-to-face situations.

If insults are ignored, or not encouraged by a like response, the problem will frequently dissipate. It still takes two to tango!

> *"Do your little bit of good where you are;*
> *it's those little bits of good put together*
> *that overwhelm the world."*
> Desmond Tutu

BENEFITS

Kindness and goodness can lead to increased well-being. It can also result in building stronger relationships, feeling good about ourselves, and making the community a better place. Even small kindnesses can make an impact far beyond what we might at first imagine.

A simple act of kindness can be both encouraging to the individual on the receiving end as well as honoring the one exhibiting the behavior. Positive and uplifting behavior can result in:

- finding favor from friends, co-workers, bosses, leaders,
- helping to avoid trouble from the unkind people in our midst,
- creating loyalty from friends and business associates,
- producing internal joy, contentment, satisfaction, and
- receiving actual physical rewards relative to job, hobbies, or other personal interests.

Goodness produces positive results and poor behavior produces negative results. If you look for trouble you can easily find it. Finding trouble in an evil world is not difficult. Insults and unkind words cause trouble to appear quickly. It can be very hard to respond with humility or patience, but the results are always far more desirable.

Personal kindness can have great impact and foster real change. It can often have a ripple effect through a family or workplace. A stone-cold business atmosphere can be warmed up with genuine kindness. Personal kindness can be a catalyst for transformative change, even in the most impersonal office environment. Genuine caring and kindnesses can reshape the nature of relationships in any setting.

In a world often driven by productivity and competition, prioritizing empathy, kindness, goodness, and compassion can create an environment in which people thrive, not just exist.

> **"Sometimes it takes only one act of kindness**
> **and caring to change a person's life."**
> Jackie Chan

KINDNESS IN ACTION

Kindness can take place anywhere. It is natural to think of it occurring with friends and family but it should extend to co-workers, acquaintances, clients, and even strangers. Examples of simple kindnesses in action might include:

1. Writing a letter of encouragement to a friend or colleague who is going through a difficult time or who has achieved something remarkable.

2. Bringing treats to share with your co-workers and expressing gratitude for their contributions and support.

3. Taking friends or co-workers out for lunch.

4. Writing encouraging messages on sticky notes and putting them on your spouse's mirror or co-worker's monitors.

5. Distributing small care packages with items like snacks or personal care products to those in need.

6. Remembering and acknowledging birthdays or special occasions with cards, cakes, or gifts.

7. Smiling at people you encounter throughout the day.

8. Complimenting others with words of encouragement.

9. Helping someone with a task, whether it's carrying something heavy or assisting them with a work assignment.

10. Being mindful of your language and avoiding gossip or speaking negatively about others.

These simple tips can be easily integrated into your daily life, allowing you to practice kindness regularly. This will have a positive impact on others while fostering a more harmonious and caring environment.

But remember your motives. Why are you doing this? It may be to help someone in need, it may be to lift the spirits of someone in a difficult time, or it may be to open up the possibility of talking seriously or confidentially with someone. It may be to simply change the atmosphere. Don't lose track of why you are doing some planned act if it is not an automatic response to a special need.

Take some time to think about how you can help others. What are your strengths and what is easy for you to do? If you are a terrible writer, sending notes might not be the place to start. If you are a good listener and find it easy to give others encouragement, that might be the place to begin.

Find a cause that you are passionate about. Seek out others who have a similar interest in that or similar causes. Recruit others with common interests to join you.

> *"Too often we underestimate the power*
> *of a touch, a smile, a kind word, a listening ear,*
> *an honest compliment, or the smallest act of caring,*
> *all of which have the potential to turn a life around."*
> Leo Buscaglia

IMPORTANCE TO AN EMPLOYER

Employers value employees who embrace kindness and goodness as a personal core value because they contribute to a positive and supportive work environment. Employees who act kindly create a caring work atmosphere. Their compassionate attitude fosters a culture of respect and understanding, making colleagues feel valued and appreciated. This leads to improved morale and a sense of unity within the workplace.

Kindness-driven employees excel in collaboration and teamwork. Their ability to listen attentively and offer help willingly will encourage effective communication and cooperation. They inspire others to adopt a similar mindset, leading to better problem-solving and ultimately increased productivity.

Customers and clients highly appreciate interactions with employees who care about their needs. Such employees will prioritize customer concerns and handle challenging situations with grace. Consequently, customers feel more satisfied and are more likely to be loyal.

Kindness as a core value also promotes strong leadership potential. Leaders who exhibit compassion and empathy tend to earn the trust and loyalty of their team members. They are approachable and make decisions with consideration for the well-being of their employees. This kind of leadership encourages personal engagement and a sense of purpose among the workforce.

Kindness-driven employees often display exceptional conflict-resolution skills. Their ability to navigate disagreements with calm understanding can lead to more effective and harmonious resolutions. This attitude is invaluable in fostering a positive work environment and maintaining healthy relationships with clients and colleagues.[0]

EXAMPLES: Kindness and Goodness Core Value Statements

1. Kindness and goodness are at the heart of who I am, guiding my actions and interactions with others.

2. I will treat everyone with compassion, empathy, and respect.

3. I will seek opportunities to perform acts of kindness every day.

4. I will be kind in order to uplift the spirits of those around me.

5. I believe in treating others with unwavering kindness.

6. I will use kindness to foster deeper connections with others in order to develop stronger and more meaningful relationships.

7. My purpose is to spread positivity and make a difference in the lives of others by embodying kindness and goodness.

8. Kindness and goodness are the guiding principles of my life, shaping my thoughts, words, and actions every day.

9. Kindness lies at the core of who I am, driving me to offer a helping hand to those in need.

10. I will strive to create a positive environment in my home and workplace by spreading goodness and joy to those around me.

MY PERSONAL CORE VALUE – Kindness and Goodness

Adopt or confirm your core value. If kindness and goodness is already a core value, or if you want to establish it as a core value, write your personal core value in the space below. You may want to use the examples above as guides to draft your Personal Core Value Statement. Make it short, succinct, and meaningful to you. Something you can easily remember.

Kindness and Goodness:

_____
_____
_____
_____
_____
_____
_____

DISCUSSION AND THOUGHT QUESTIONS

1. Do you find it easy or hard to offer others kindness, encouragement, or compassion? Why is that?

2. How has an act of kindness from someone else positively impacted your life and how did it make you feel?

3. How do you typically act when someone is kind to you?

4. Can you remember a time when you did something kind or good for someone else? What happened?

5. If you observed someone being unkind to another, how would you try to diffuse or resolve the situation?

6. If you experienced someone being good or kind to another, how could you encourage their behavior?

7. Bob Proctor said, *"The law of prosperity is generosity. If you want more, give more."* Do you think this is true? Why?

8. Can you recall when someone's act of goodness inspired you to do the same for others? Was there a ripple effect?

9. Reflect on a situation in which kindness was not exhibited. How might kindness have yielded a different outcome?

10. Have you ever experienced the consequences of not acting with kindness? How did it affect your relationships?

NOTES

I want to do the following:

a. _____
b. _____
c. _____
d. _____

I want to remember:

a. _____
b. _____
c. _____
d. _____

Action Challenge: Perform three random acts of kindness this week, without expecting anything in return. Observe how these acts affect your own mood and the reactions of others. Consider how you can integrate more intentional kindness into your daily life.

Chapter 10
Compassion

COMPASSION LIFE PRINCIPLE:
I will have compassion for others.

"We must always have compassion,
even when it is difficult or inconvenient."
Mother Teresa

GENERAL

Mercy and compassion are important virtues because they help build stronger relationships and make the environment a more pleasant place. They can also be a source of comfort and hope for those who are suffering.

Mercy is a virtue that is often associated with compassion, kindness, and forgiveness. It is the willingness to forgo punishment or revenge even when it may be deserved. Mercy might be described as forgiving someone who has wronged you, not punishing someone who deserves correction, helping someone who is suffering, or assisting someone who is in need.

A common focus of wisdom sayings about compassion is that those who show such characteristics will receive them in return. There is a proverb (author unknown) that says, "*Compassion is the inspiration of the soul and where there is compassion even the most wicked desires remain relatively harmless.*" Compassion is certainly a quality that is generated by a life well-lived or a soul that is well nurtured.

In today's environment of toxic social media, compassion and mercy seem to be lost or at least well-disguised. The easy response for the faceless agitator is confrontation. When social interaction is performed behind a digital mask it opens the door for uncaring and mean-spirited people to say anything they want without regard for decency, truth, or compassion. It's like the petulant child in his closed room yelling at his mom in the hall – he is often out of control and is likely to say whatever comes to mind. But the atmosphere quickly changes when Mom opens the door and enters the room.

Anonymity has opened the door for
a great deal of unneeded and unacceptable speech.

Definitions

Mercy and compassion are both positive characteristics that involve feeling concern for others. However, there are several differences between these two attributes.

> *Mercy* is defined as "the compassionate treatment of those in distress, especially when it is within one's power to punish or harm them." It is often associated with benevolence and kindness. For example, a judge might show mercy to a defendant who has committed a crime by giving him a lighter sentence than is deserved.
>
> *Compassion* is defined as the "sympathetic concern for the sufferings or misfortunes of others." It is often associated with empathy and understanding which reflects a true desire to help. For example, a person might show compassion for a friend who is going through a difficult time by listening to them, offering support, helping them fix a problem, or providing resources to overcome difficulties. (Merriam-Webster)

Mercy might be said to be more about giving someone what they do not deserve, while compassion is more about feeling for someone and giving them help. Mercy is feeling pity for someone who is suffering. It is given from a position of having the power or authority to help while compassion is associated more with being aware of, sensitive to, and feeling the hurt of another person. Thus, mercy can be shown to anyone regardless of the situation while compassion is giving help to the less fortunate or somebody who has been wronged.

When we provide mercy, we give others a second chance. When we give compassion, we directly help to ease someone's suffering. Together they bring a balanced dynamic to society.

In practice, there is often little difference between these two terms. To show mercy is to pardon someone or treat them leniently because you feel merciful. If you have compassion there is a deeper awareness of the suffering accompanied with a true desire to help. For simplicity in the remaining body of this chapter we will use the term compassion to represent both these attributes.

> ### *Compassion is a fundamental trait*
> ### *of the human condition.*

Why is compassion important?

There are generally four categories of compassion. One is the simple act of forgiving someone who may have wronged you in some way. A second aspect is the decision not to punish an offender who deserves correction or some form of penalty. Third is the act of feeling and showing concern for someone who is suffering. Finally there is giving or arranging help for someone in need.

Compassion can help heal relationships, build bridges, provide justice, or create an acceptable result that society will support. Some specific examples may be helpful:

> *Relationships.* When we forgive someone who has wronged us, we are giving them the opportunity to make amends and rebuild trust. This can help repair and restore relationships that have been damaged by conflict or hurt.

> *Building Bridges.* Compassion can help break down barriers that exist between people and create a more inclusive and welcoming environment. We send a message that we are willing to accept them for who they are, even when they are different from us. For example a local charity might organize cultural events and encourage dialogue between different

ethnic groups. Or, several members of a diverse neighborhood might organize a block party.

> *Force for Good.* Compassion and selfless service to others can create better communities. Compassion can be a powerful force for good in the world. It can help and encourage a more caring community in which people are treated with dignity and respect, diversity is lauded, and the focus is on peace and contentment rather than on selfish desires for power, advancement, or gain.

Compassion is an important personal characteristic that can fuel hope in a dark world. It is choosing to ignore inconsequential events, avoiding hurtful words, and responding with kindness.

Compassion is a reflection of the soul.

LOVE COMPASSION

There is an instruction from the Jewish Torah that says we should "act justly, love mercy, and walk humbly with our God." (Micah 6:8) This puts the concept of mercy or compassion in some important company. One might argue that if someone kept just these three instructions in life, they would be right with God, right with man, and right with self. Who is left?

One could feel very good about a life that was just, compassionate, and lived with humility. Before you dismiss this concept, what do you think is missing from these three characteristics? What is missing if you want a life of satisfaction and contentment? A broad interpretation of these three terms would cover a great deal of ground, with very little missing.

What does that tell us about compassion? I think it is easy to conclude that compassion should be a foundational character trait. It should highly influence the way we want to live and be particularly effective in our interpersonal relationships.

Be compassionate if you want to receive compassion

It is logical to assume that those who are compassionate to others would probably receive like treatment in return. Think about your feelings and emotions when you are treated with compassion in some unfortunate situation. It is natural to treat others well when you have been treated well. It may simply be giving someone a second chance. You remember acts of kindness you have received when you have an opportunity for reciprocal treatment.

Compassion is important. It might be the simple words, "I'm sorry. Please forgive me." These words can have significant impact on others. Unkind, unforgiving, callous, or harsh treatment of others usually comes back to haunt the one who refuses or ignores the appropriate compassionate response. Life has a way of providing rewards or judgments for good and bad behavior.

There is always someone watching! Your behavior at home, school, work, gym, and the store is being observed and evaluated constantly by watching eyes.

If you were at a store and the clerk treated you unkindly or without compassion, how likely are you to return? Do you just ignore the offense? Many will reconsider using that store again. Being inconsiderate and acting without compassion as the representative of any organization can have long-lasting consequences. Companies that pride themselves on customer service will often terminate employees who do not conform to certain levels of compassionate behavior.

If you want to receive compassion
you need to give it away!

What would you do?

Jack regularly led retreat workshops for improving one's life, generally focused on a particular character trait. The week-long workshops were always well attended. Last year Jack had a new and different situation crop up in one of his retreats. Someone was stealing things from other participants.

On the second day of the workshop the participants realized that someone was stealing from them and they immediately informed Jack, but he was not willing to take any action to identify the thief. The stealing occurred again the next day, but the thief was seen and the participants informed John of the thief's identity.

Again, Jack ignored the whole situation and did nothing. Finally, the group objected and said that they could not go on with the workshop when they knew a thief was likely ransacking their rooms while they were meeting together. Jack finally agreed to do something. He asked everyone to meet together and he pointed at the thief and said, "*This poor soul has stolen things because he does not understand that he does not need to steal to receive help. There is nothing he needs to take from anyone. He simply does not understand that we have such a richness of character that we can afford to be compassionate.*"

Jack went on to say that the workshop would end the next day and he asked all attendees to do him a favor. He asked the group to give the offender whatever he needed so that he understood that "together we have enough to support each other." The thief was so moved that he broke down in tears and returned everything he had stolen.[3]

This story illustrates how compassion can impact lives. Not only was the offender rehabilitated, but those who suffered potential loss participated in the restoration process.

What would you have done in these circumstances? Would your first thought have been to offer help? Frankly, it would not have been mine, and I'm sure it would not even have occurred to me. This tells me I need to give more thought to my compassion button.

> ***Showing compassion is a sign***
> ***of character and grace.***

WARNINGS

Warnings about the lack of kindness or compassion typically indicate that not doing what is right will bring some form of "disaster and destruction." On the other hand, one who does what is right will receive benefits or rewards. This is the typical idea of most wisdom sayings: good produces good and bad produces bad. Kindness begets kindness and evil begets evil. You receive or harvest what you sow, thus, the compassionate will receive compassion in return. The cruel or unkind are likely to receive the same inconsiderate treatment in return. It's almost a law of nature!

If you are not prone to being compassionate, you may want to take a hard look at yourself and your core values. Your actions or non-action can have significant consequences to yourself and those around you. We are no longer islands in a large world. Someone is watching and listening to everything we do and say (family, friends, even strangers). We are constantly being observed by others.

ADVICE

People who insult the poor, ignore their needs, and refuse to help the disadvantaged may incur the indignation of those who oppose oppression and the inconsiderate treatment of others. Why? Because the disadvantaged and needy generally don't have a voice and when they do speak they are often ignored. If you are apathetic towards the real human needs of the poor and disadvantaged you may lose opportunities that might have otherwise been offered.

What does it really mean to be compassionate? The very simplistic "Golden Rule" is a good benchmark. Treat others the way you would want to be treated if you were in their situation. Be caring toward others, no matter their attitudes. This means you would be kind, gentle, and patient regardless of their words or actions. We can probably never be perfect but that should not prevent us from trying.

One who is compassionate often wears that attribute like a suit of clothes. They not only speak about compassion, they do something meaningful to help. Compassion defines them. It does not come to the surface only under special circumstances but is there continually. Someone with the core value of compassion feels "clothed" in it and everyone else sees it.

Someone with the *gift* of compassion will often suffer internally along with the one experiencing the real hurt. True compassion is not ever half-way, part-time, or a matter of convenience, but is fully on alert at all times. Those without such a *gift* may not have that inner turmoil, but we all should have concern and watch for opportunities to act. We should all be ready to offer a helping hand when it is needed.

> *"Mercy is not just a virtue, it is a way of life."*
> Martin Luther King Jr.

How can we develop compassion?

The development of compassion is an ongoing process and requires consistent cultivation. Through regular thought, practice, and real involvement, you can deepen your capacity for compassion. But the key is involvement. It must be an active concern if you want compassion to be a personal core value.

It is important that you notice the suffering of others and attempt to understand their perspective in order to be helpful. This understanding may not come naturally. You may not have a sense of empathy for others. Developing empathy will normally take time and real intentionality. You must allow yourself to be moved emotionally by the situations you observe (pity, sympathy, sorrow). If you have observed and been moved by a situation, the next step is taking some appropriate action – demonstrating care or concern by being helpful.

Practice is the key!

The key to developing a compassionate spirit is participation. Get involved with serving others. If you are serious about trying to develop or improve your compassion, the best course of action is to participate in some activity of serving others. There is nothing better than regular exposure to people who are less fortunate to get your compassion juices flowing. It does not have to be a dramatic experience. Start small and work up to bigger environments as your senses and skills become better prepared to handle difficult situations.

Remember

Being compassionate can be challenging. Other personal skills may be needed in order to be effective. It can be difficult to be compassionate when we are not used to it. Compassion may not be our first reaction when real need confronts us. It can also be difficult when we are angry, hurt, or when we do not understand why someone has wronged us. But wisdom says that we are called to love mercy and offer compassion to others in need.

> *"The true measure of a society's greatness*
> *is how it treats its weakest members."*
> Mahatma Gandhi

PERSONAL BENEFITS

There are some general benefits that compassionate people receive that are somewhat universal in nature. You should feel good about yourself, your life, or your own personal circumstances. Being compassionate can provide a general sense of satisfaction and contentment. There can also be real feelings of contributing to society. In addition, there are other feelings and emotions that are more personal in nature:

1. *Joy:* Feelings of deep satisfaction come from helping others and making a real impact on their lives. It is a feeling of connection and knowing you are part of something bigger or more important than yourself. It is a feeling of hope and optimism.

2. *Happiness:* Temporary feelings of pleasure, gladness, or delight.

3. *Contentment:* You may feel content that you have truly made a difference. You may come to realize how fortunate you are which can create feelings of gratitude for your own personal situation.

4. *Satisfaction:* You can be grateful for what you have accomplished for others. This can produce a positive outlook on life and make your own problems seem minor.

5. *Peace:* You can reasonably expect to receive compassion in return, especially from those you treated well or those with whom you

worked in serving others. Caring people are admired and loved. Many will come to your aid if help is needed.

6. *Relationships:* You can connect with others who share your compassionate feelings and create lasting relationships with others who have the same perspectives and core values. You can also form deep relationships with those who you are assisting.

TIPS FOR SERVING OTHERS

1. Show respect and friendliness. Smile and make eye contact.
2. Show concern by sharing the human touch and appropriate body language.
3. Be a good listener. Respond to simple needs or wants. Show you care.
4. Communicate in a gentle and unassuming voice.
5. Talk to the lonely, homebound, or distressed.
6. Write a personal note of encouragement.
7. Offer a helping hand where needed and follow through.
8. Carry $5 gift cards for needy people or strangers.
9. Babysit for a single mom.
10. Help someone who is seriously struggling.
11. Donate money or work or at a local food bank.
12. Mentor someone who needs help making good decisions.

IMPORTANCE TO AN EMPLOYER

Employers highly value employees who exhibit compassion. Such individuals bring a unique set of behaviors to the workplace that can positively impact the work environment and contribute to the atmosphere of the workplace.

Compassionate employees are empathetic and understanding towards their colleagues. This fosters a sense of unity and support among team members as they feel cared for in times of both personal and professional challenges. Compassionate employees are more likely to lend a helping hand, creating a collaborative atmosphere where everyone works together toward common goals.

The compassionate employee's ability to listen, show genuine concern, and offer assistance (without judgment) enhances communication and conflict resolution within the workplace.

Employees with compassion are more likely to provide exceptional customer service. They genuinely care about the satisfaction and happiness of customers, leading to stronger relationships and increased loyalty.[0]

EXAMPLES: Compassion Core Value Statements

1. I value compassion. I will seek to understand the struggles of others and offer a helping hand without judgment.

2. I believe in treating others with kindness and compassion, recognizing their inherent worth and dignity.

3. Compassion guides my actions, inspiring me to prioritize the well-being of others.

4. Mercy leads me to forgive others and myself, in order to foster an environment of peace and understanding.

5. I am committed to supporting charitable causes and volunteering my time in my community.

6. I will offer compassion, empowering and uplifting those around me to reach their full potential.

7. I will extend forgiveness and grace, recognizing that we all make mistakes and can learn and grow from them.

8. I will approach conflicts with a compassionate mindset, seeking resolution and understanding rather than confrontation.

9. Mercy and compassion shape how I interact with the world and contribute to a more caring society.

MY PERSONAL CORE VALUE – Compassion

Adopt or confirm your core value. If compassion is already a core value, or if you want to establish it as a core value, write your personal core value statement in the space below. You may want to use the examples above as guides to draft your Personal Core Value

Statement. Make it short, succinct, and meaningful to you. Something you can easily remember.

Compassion:

_____
_____
_____
_____
_____
_____

DISSCUSSION AND THOUGHT QUESTIONS

1. There is a wise saying, "If you want to receive compassion you need to give it away!" Do you think this is true? Why?

2. What causes you to exercise your compassion? Why?

3. Does the hurt of others trigger your compassion?

4. Do you think apathy, entitlement, or the laziness of needy people should slow the need for compassion? Why? Why not?

5. Who do you think deserves mercy or compassion? Why? Who would you help? Who would you refuse to help? Why?

6. Some believe that mercy should not be shown to anyone that has not been merciful. Would you agree or disagree? Why?

7. What if the one in need of mercy or compassion is inherently wicked and evil? What would you do? Why?

8. How do you personally compare or relate mercy and compassion to the concepts of justice and forgiveness?

9. Can you think of a situation in which you found it challenging to be compassionate? What were the circumstances?

10. Think of a time when someone showed you compassion. How did it make you feel? What effect did it have on you?

11. Is it necessary to strike a balance between compassion, accountability, and fairness?

NOTES

I want to do the following:

a. _____

b. _____

c. _____

I want to remember:

a. _____

b. _____

c. _____

Action Challenge: Think about someone in your life who is going through a difficult time. Reach out to them with compassion and offer your support, whether it's a listening ear, a helping hand, or a heartfelt message. Reflect on how this act of compassion strengthens your connection and theirs.

Chapter 11
Equality

EQUALITY LIFE PRINCIPLE:
Treating others with equity and equality.

"Injustice anywhere is a threat to justice everywhere."
Martin Luther King Jr.

GENERAL

Equality refers to the principle that all individuals should have the same rights, opportunities, and treatment, regardless of their background or circumstances. It emphasizes fairness and the absence of discrimination or bias.

While the concept of equality can have different interpretations and applications across various subjects, it basically entails the concept of non-discrimination. Equality ensures that every individual has the same fundamental rights and freedoms, similar to our Constitution which indicates that we all have the right to life, liberty, and the pursuit of happiness. You have probably heard that phrase before! We should not be treated differently based on factors such as race, gender, religion, nationality, social status, etc.

Equality means we all have equal access to opportunities, resources, and social benefits, regardless of our background or inherent personal characteristics. This applies to all aspects of life: education, employment, healthcare, essential services, etc. Equality means there is a level playing field for everyone. It requires the elimination of discrimination and prejudice. It promotes the concept that all individuals are to be treated with dignity and respect.

While equality focuses on treating everyone equally, it also acknowledges that different individuals may require different levels of support or accommodations to achieve true fairness. Equity addresses historical disadvantages and the existence of systemic barriers. The goal is to provide all individuals with what is necessary for them to thrive and be successful.

Treating others equally aligns with the pursuit of social justice, which tries to rectify systemic inequalities within our culture. It means that certain systems that continually perpetuate inequality need to be modified in order to produce a more equitable result.

Equality today is an ongoing process that involves addressing historical, social, and structural inequalities, while continually striving to ensure equal treatment for <u>all</u> individuals.

> *"We should judge individuals*
> *not by the color of their skin,*
> *but by the content of their character."*
> Martin Luther King Jr.

Importance

Equality is important to each of us because it reflects our values and principles as individual people. If someone can be treated unfairly today for having red hair, then tomorrow you and I can be treated unfairly because we live in the state of xxx. If that thought shocks you, it should. Laws and customs can be changed by those in power to enhance or discriminate against any chosen target. What is fair can be defined by those with power to change laws or accomplish their demands with force.

Equality is rooted in the principles of fairness, justice, and respect for the inherent worth and dignity of every individual. Embracing equality as a core value means you recognize the intrinsic value of all human beings, regardless of their differences.

Equality will encourage you to empathize with others and understand their experiences, challenges, and needs. By valuing equality, we cultivate compassion which fosters stronger connections with others and creates a more inclusive and supportive environment.

We are <u>not</u> suggesting that all people be treated the same or that high character or performance not be rewarded. Treating others with fairness and equality does not mean discriminating against high performing individuals.

When we treat others with equality we create an atmosphere of trust and mutual respect. It helps build stronger and more meaningful relationships as respect promotes open communication and cooperation. This enhances the quality of both personal and business relationships.

Treating others with equality may require challenging your biases and prejudices. You may have to expand your perspectives and understanding of reality.

> *"Treating others equally is not just a moral duty,*
> *but a reflection of our own character."*
> Michelle Obama

How to practice

What should you do to be considered acceptable in the area of equality? What types of actions or activities represent positive influences? Generally any act that respects others and treats them fairly would qualify. It does not necessarily mean special treatment unless you are trying to correct some inherent wrong.

You can practice equality in relationships by any of the following:

Listening: Listen to others without judgment, genuinely valuing their perspectives. Respect their autonomy. Give everyone an equal opportunity to express themselves and be heard.

Fairness: Make decisions based on objective criteria, fairness, and merit rather than favoring certain individuals or groups over others. Treat everyone equally in matters such as promotions, opportunities, and resource allocations.

Bias: Actively work at challenging and overcoming bias. Recognize that *preconceived* notions can lead to unfair treatment. Make a conscious effort to treat individuals based on their personal merits, abilities, and character rather than making assumptions based on stereotypes.

Language: Use inclusive language that does not exclude or marginalize anyone. Be mindful of the impact of words and actions and avoiding discriminatory or derogatory language.

Influence: Use your privilege, position, or influence to make your position and concerns known to others. Stand up against discrimination! Work towards creating a fair and just environment.

> **"Our true greatness lies in how we treat others,**
> **not in how others treat us."**
> Pope Francis

OUR BIAS

We all have our own internal bias toward people and ideas. We may be aware of that bias or we may be ignorant of its existence. Discovering and dealing with our own internal prejudices is an important and ongoing process of personal growth.

Bias can exist in the smallest of matters or it can be so great that others are hurt. Thus, you need to take steps to identify your own personal prejudices. Here are some suggestions that can help you improve in this area:

Self-examination: Engage in self-reflection to become aware of your own biases. Think about your beliefs, attitudes, and assumptions about different social groups and identities. Ask yourself honest questions about any stereotypes or prejudices you may hold.

Awareness: Educate yourself about diverse cultures, perspectives, and experiences. Seek out resources that challenge known stereotypes. Actively seek to expand your knowledge and understanding of how marginalized communities are treated and the impact inequality has on their lives.

Engagement: Participate in open and respectful conversations with others about diversity, equality, or social issues. Seek diverse viewpoints and engage in constructive discussions to challenge your own biases and broaden your understanding. Be open to other perspectives and be willing to consider and evaluate new viewpoints.

Assumptions: When you catch yourself making assumptions or generalizations about individuals or groups, stop and question your thinking. Challenge your inherent stereotypes!

Decision-Making: Analyze your decision-making processes to ensure fairness and equal treatment of others. Do any biases currently influence your judgments or actions? Strive to make decisions based on objective criteria.

Feedback: Be open to feedback from others and create a safe place for individuals to provide input on your words and behavior. Encourage trusted friends, colleagues, or mentors to provide constructive feedback on any biases they observe in your words or actions. Hearing negative feedback is not always comfortable. Unless you are mature, this can be a difficult process. If you choose to seek feedback, promise yourself not to challenge anything you are told.

Summary: Recognize that addressing bias is an ongoing process. Remember, you are not likely to erase it entirely, but try to become more aware of it and actively work to mitigate its influence on your thoughts, actions, and decision-making processes.

> **"Prejudice is a burden that confuses the past,**
> **threatens the future, and renders the present inaccessible."**
> Maya Angelou

BE OPEN

Being open-minded plays a crucial role in identifying your bias and understanding diversity. It allows you to approach experiences and cultures with curiosity rather than judgment. It enables you to recognize that there are multiple ways of viewing the world and that your own perspective is not necessarily the only valid one. By embracing and experiencing different perspectives you can gain a deeper understanding of diverse backgrounds and challenge any preconceived notions or biases you may have.

In today's world it is easy to adopt generalizations that can be unfair and inaccurate. It is important to understand that all individuals are shaped by their own history of experiences. You should seek to approach others without preconceived judgments, treating them as individuals rather than as representatives of a particular group.

Open-mindedness enables you to put yourself in the shoes of others. You will quickly understand those shoes don't fit well because they involve a different social and cultural lifestyle. By understanding diverse experiences, you can develop a deeper empathy for others and treat them with greater compassion and fairness because you have a truer understanding of who they are.

> *"Open-minded people don't care to be right,*
> *they care to understand."*
> Unknown

CHALLENGES

Overcoming tendencies to treat others unequally requires conscious effort and a commitment to do what is right. Achieving improvement begins with awareness. We all have bias as described above and we need to deal with how we handle our prejudices.

Taking on our own bias can be extremely challenging. Serious re-education may be required if you hold deep-seated prejudices. But it is imperative that you understand the barriers that others face and the impact of inequality on their lives. Questioning assumptions or positions you may hold because you were raised on a diet of misinformation or discrimination can be very difficult unless you are determined to be intentional. Remember this is a *decision* you make!

Active involvement may be what you need, but that may be a difficult decision on your part. You will only be intentional about this subject when you decide it is something you want to do. It is probably better to begin with small steps until you have a better understanding of what you are doing.

Recognize that overcoming deeply ingrained prejudices takes time and ongoing effort. Engage in regular self-examination to monitor your progress. Be open to learning from your mistakes and commit to personal growth in the pursuit of treating others equally.

> ***"Equality begins with the next person you talk to. Equality is not a privilege to be earned, but a right to be respected."***
> Unknown

BENEFITS

Embracing equality fosters authentic connections with others. By treating individuals with equality, you create a foundation of trust and mutual understanding within your relationships.

Practicing equality encourages open and honest communication. It creates a safe space for others to express themselves without fear of judgment or discrimination. The result is healthy and effective communication. Others will trust what you have to say when you demonstrate attitudes of respect and dignity.

Supporting equality in the community involves bringing diverse groups together. Your fair and equal treatment of diverse groups can help address systemic inequalities and create a more just and desirable environment in your area. This can contribute to reducing social disparities that foster distrust and even hatred.

A community that supports equality benefits from improved quality of life for everyone. Equal access to education, healthcare, housing, and jobs can lead to increased well-being, improved social mobility, and a more inclusive community, impacting the lives of everyone in the area.

Supporting equality demonstrates a commitment to social responsibility and fairness.

> ***"We are all equally valuable, equally human, and equally deserving of respect and dignity."***
> Desmond Tutu

PRACTICAL TIPS

Here are some very simple and easy-to-implement tips to demonstrate and practice equality in your daily life:

1. Avoid assumptions: Don't make assumptions based on someone's gender, race, ethnicity, or background. Treat each person as an individual with unique experiences and qualities. Get to know them.

2. Challenge stereotypes: Speak up when you encounter stereotypes. Help others understand the harmful impact of misconceptions.

3. Support diverse voices: Encourage and amplify diverse voices or causes, especially those that are underrepresented or marginalized. Advocate for diversity in your workplace, school, and community whenever you have the opportunity.

4. Educate yourself: Continuously educate yourself about different cultures and social issues to create real understanding of problems.

5. Intervene: If you witness discrimination or unfair treatment, be willing to step in and support the affected person.

6. Volunteer: Contribute your time and skills to organizations that work towards promoting equality and social justice.

7. Inclusive: Make sure *everyone* feels welcome and valued in your social circles and gatherings. Be mindful of the language you use.

Remember, practicing equality is an ongoing effort that requires consistent action and an open mind. Small actions can often make a big difference in promoting a more equitable society.

IMPORTANCE TO AN EMPLOYER

Leaders set the tone in any business. Effective leaders do not ignore or shy away from diversity. Diversity can be the catalyst for innovative solutions. The world is diverse! Good leaders hire good people regardless of color, creed, gender, or lifestyle. Today's world is very competitive and the intent of every good leader should be to hire the very best people possible. Diversity is often a key to a successful work environment because it brings together different ideas and customs that can produce change, innovation, and creativity.

It is also important to provide a safe and comfortable workplace where everyone has the opportunity to grow and advance. If you practice discrimination in today's world you risk being in conflict with moral, local, and national laws. If you want to be an effective leader, you must deal with the diversity of a global workplace.

Supporting equality in your workplace can create many benefits. Here are three of the real advantages you may experience:

- *Positive Environment:* Equality in the workplace fosters a positive and inclusive work environment. Employees feel valued and respected leading to higher job satisfaction, increased productivity, and improved morale.

- *Innovation:* Embracing diversity encourages new perspectives and ideas. When individuals from different backgrounds and identities are treated equally, they feel comfortable sharing their unique insights.

- *Employee Attraction and Retention:* Employers who actively support equality are more attractive to diverse talent. By valuing equality, you can help create a diverse and inclusive workforce, attracting top talent from different backgrounds.[0]

"The only way to create a just society is to
treat every individual with fairness and equality."
Nelson Mandela

EXAMPLES: Equality Core Value Statements

Following are sample core value statements that you might choose to adopt if you want equality as one of your personal core values:

1. I believe in treating all individuals with respect, fairness, and compassion, regardless of their background or identity.

2. I value diversity and inclusivity, striving to create opportunities where everyone is respected.

3. Equality will guide my actions and decisions in both personal and professional aspects of life.

4. I am committed to challenging discrimination and promoting a more just and equitable environment for all.

5. I believe in advocating for equal access to resources, ensuring that everyone has a fair chance to succeed.

6. My core value of equality drives me to speak up against injustice and to support marginalized communities.

7. I aspire to be an ally to those facing discrimination, using my position to support positive change.

8. I prioritize breaking down barriers and working toward a world in which everyone is treated with dignity and respect.

9. I support recognizing and celebrating the unique contributions and strengths of each individual.

10. I am dedicated to educating myself and others about social issues and will work towards dismantling systemic inequalities.

11. I strive to create a personal and work environment that values diversity and provides equal opportunities to all individuals.

12. I believe in building bridges of understanding among diverse groups in order to foster unity and harmony in my community.

MY PERSONAL CORE VALUE – Equality

Adopt or confirm your core value. If equality is already a core value, or if you want to establish it as a core value, write your personal core value in the space below. You may want to use the examples above as guides to draft your Personal Core Value Statement. Make it short, succinct, and meaningful to you. Something you can easily remember.

Equality:

_____
_____
_____
_____
_____
_____
_____
_____

DISCUSSION AND THOUGHT QUESTIONS

1. What does diversity mean to you personally? How do you define it?

2. How does embracing diversity contribute to a more inclusive and equitable workplace or community?

3. Can you share an experience in which you felt unfairly treated due to your race, gender, or other aspects of your identity? How did it impact you?

4. What biases or stereotypes do you think exist in your life experience that hinders equal treatment for all individuals? How do you think they could be overcome?

5. Have you ever caught yourself making assumptions about someone based on their appearance or background? How can we become more aware of our own biases and work to eliminate them?

6. How can one encourage open and respectful dialogue about diversity and equality within family, community, or organization?

7. What specific policies or practices do you believe should be in place to ensure equal opportunities for all individuals? Why do you think they are important?

8. Have you ever witnessed someone being treated unfairly or experiencing discrimination? How did you respond and what did you learn from that experience?

9. What role do you believe education plays in promoting diversity and equality?

10. How can we foster understanding among individuals from diverse backgrounds? What activities could be implemented that would promote better understanding?

NOTES

I want to do the following:

a. _____

b. _____

c. _____

I want to remember:

a. _____

b. _____

c. _____

Action Challenge: Reflect on your attitudes and behaviors toward people from different backgrounds or circumstances. Identify one way you can actively promote equality and equity in your daily life, whether it's advocating for fair treatment or supporting initiatives that level the playing field.

Chapter 12
Personal Growth
Learning

WISDOM LIFE PRINCIPLE:
I will actively seek knowledge
and understanding.

*"The beautiful thing about learning is
that no one can take it away from you."*
B.B. King

GENERAL

Personal growth in its broadest sense can encompasses emotional, intellectual, physical, and spiritual aspects of your life. It involves developing your potential, enhancing personal qualities, and striving for personal fulfillment. It does not have to be a broad approach to learning; it can be specifically directed toward areas of growth or learning that have particular interest to you.

There are many ways to expand your knowledge: books, classes, seminars, workshops, podcasts, and internships – the list of opportunities is endless. It can include pursuing academics, professional skills, hobbies, or just personal interests.

While learning can be a part of the process, your personal growth extends beyond the act of simply gaining knowledge. Personal growth involves self-reflection, study, setting goals, and taking action. It may involve personal transformation, changing attitudes or beliefs, developing resilience, or improving relationships.

*"The more that you read, the more things you will know.
The more you learn the more places you'll go."*
Dr. Seuss

The internal and personal benefit of accomplishing goals through personal knowledge and understanding can be deeply rewarding. A deep sense of satisfaction from such success can fuel accomplishments in many aspects of your life.

Key aspects of learning

Being committed to learning and personal growth produces many benefits. Here are some key aspects of personal growth:

Change. Embracing personal growth as a core value fosters a mindset of continuous improvement. It helps you acquire knowledge and abilities. This enables you to adapt to changing circumstances and stay relevant in a world in which technology is exploding and changing how you act, work, and even how you think.

Confidence. By actively seeking knowledge, you gain confidence which will empower you to shape both your personal and professional career path. Such confidence comes from a real understanding of your capabilities and the desire to tackle new challenges with a sense of self-assurance.

Fulfillment. Engaging in growth activities that align with your interests and passions can bring a deep sense of personal fulfillment. This allows you explore your potential, discover new talents, and pursue meaningful life goals.

Resilience. Personal knowledge and understanding enables you to overcome obstacles more effectively. By continuously acquiring new knowledge and skills you are more able to manage uncertainty or bounce back from difficulties. You will not easily be discouraged and you can continue to learn and grow in the face of challenges.

Opportunities. Learning opens up a world of opportunities. It enhances your qualifications and increases your chances of discovering new avenues for career and personal development. It will also allow you to discover new interests and interesting people.

Problem-Solving. A commitment to learning and growth enhances your problem-solving abilities. As you accumulate knowledge and diverse experiences you develop a broader range of abilities to tackle more complex problems. You become more adept at critical thinking, decision-making, and finding innovative solutions to problems.

Improved Relationships. Personal growth enhances your interpersonal skills and communication abilities. These skills contribute to more meaningful relationships with family, friends, and co-workers. Improved communication skills are valuable in all walks of life.

> **"Education is not preparation for life;**
> **education is life itself."**
> John Dewey

HOW TO DEVELOP

There are a number of things you can do to develop this core value. First and perhaps most important is to adopt a positive mindset. A mindset that believes in the capacity for growth, improvement, and learning is a real advantage when you face a new or challenging situation. If you are willing to embrace challenges, personal improvement is much easier.

Defining learning goals that align with your personal interests is a practical step toward addressing personal development. You need to understand what you want to accomplish. Breaking down your goals into actionable steps and creating a plan for achieving them can be of significant value.

In order to grow in understanding you should *actively* seek out learning opportunities: books, online courses, seminars or webinars. Learning opportunities don't necessarily happen on some pre-determined schedule. You need to be intentional about what you want to pursue and how you want to achieve your growth.

You can leverage technology and digital resources to enhance your learning ability. Explore online platforms, educational apps, or podcasts that provide opportunities for self-paced learning and exposure to new ideas or new skills.

Learning activities often provide opportunities for connecting with other people who share similar interests. Building strong and diverse relationships increases the likelihood of career growth through referrals when new opportunities occur.

Surround yourself with individuals who value learning and personal growth. Seek out mentors and like-minded individuals who can inspire and support your learning goals. Mentors can help you navigate challenges and problems, as well as accelerate your learning. They can often tell you things you do not see for yourself.

Engage in meaningful conversations, with others to enhance your knowledge. Join online forums or social media groups focused on your areas of interest. Engaging with others who share your passion for learning can provide great opportunities for collaboration.

After you have obtained knowledge or improved your skills, put them to work. Apply the skills you acquire to real-life situations and opportunities. Implement what you've learned in practical settings whether it's in your family, work, or community.

Adopting these behaviors can actively increase the speed of your learning process. They should become part of your identity and influence the choices you make to continually learn and grow.

> *"I am always doing that which I cannot do,*
> *in order that I may learn how to do it."*
> Pablo Picasso

Life alignment

Personal growth should reflect a commitment to be the best you can be as a person. It should align with the value of investing in yourself. Prioritizing learning and growth should also be consistent with your other core values and life goals.

By choosing learning opportunities that are in line with your core values you ensure that your life path is consistent with your life goals and view of the future.

Career advancement

Personal growth has a strong connection to career advancement and can significantly increase job opportunities. The three primary reasons for this are:

1. Skill Development

Embracing learning and personal growth allows you to acquire new skills and enhance existing ones. These skills directly contribute to your career by making you more capable and marketable in your field. As you become more knowledgeable and skilled you become eligible for higher-level positions and increased responsibilities. This leads directly to enhancing your career competence.

Continuous learning ensures that you stay up-to-date with the latest trends and best practices in your industry. It enhances professional competence, making the learner a valuable asset to employers. As employees at any level become more competent they become better equipped to handle more complex tasks and challenges. This will open doors to career growth opportunities.

2. Adaptability to Change

Personal growth assists in adaptability, agility, and flexibility. In today's rapidly evolving work environment, managing change is a crucial job requirement. Individuals who actively seek out new skills are better equipped to embrace change and thrive in ever-changing work environments. Your ability to adapt will often position you ahead of those who reject or fear change.

Being flexible will create recognition of your abilities. You will naturally stand out in your job or career, thus, you are more likely to be recognized by supervisors and colleagues. This increased visibility can lead to opportunities and increased responsibility.

3. Job Satisfaction

When you are actively engaged in your own development you experience a sense of personal fulfillment and accomplishment. You will feel more challenged and motivated in your roles. This sense of progress increases overall job satisfaction and reduces the likelihood of feeling stagnant or unfulfilled in your work life.

> **"The only person who is educated is the one who has learned how to learn and change."**
> Carl Rogers

PRACTICAL TIPS

Here are some simple tips for practicing or developing the core value of personal growth:

1. Goals: Define achievable goals for different areas of your life.

2. Read: Dedicate time to reading books, articles, or blogs that expand your knowledge.

3. Skill: Choose a small skill you've always wanted to acquire and commit to mastering it.

4. Feedback: Encourage constructive feedback from peers or colleagues to identify areas for improvement.

5. Networking: Engage with people to gain fresh perspectives and expand your personal and professional network.

6. Courses: Enroll in online courses or workshops to enhance your knowledge and skills.

7. Health: Choose one particular health activity to improve, such as regular exercise, a balanced diet, or adequate sleep.

8. Time Management: Work on your time management skills to maximize productivity and create time for personal growth.

CHALLENGES

Implementing personal growth activities can bring certain challenges. Finding time for learning can be difficult amidst other commitments and responsibilities. Work, family, and other obligations may limit the amount of time you have available. Balancing your schedule and prioritizing learning will require careful planning.

It can be difficult to maintain a regular learning routine, especially when faced with distractions or competing priorities. The abundance of information and learning resources available can be overwhelming. It can be difficult to identify the most relevant and best alternatives to pursue. Filtering through the vast amount of information and selecting the most valuable resources can be a significant challenge.

Fear of failure can hinder progress and discourage you from pursuing new learning opportunities. Overcoming this fear and embracing a growth mindset is crucial for making real progress. Without a support system it can be challenging to stay motivated to your personal goals. The absence of mentors or other peers may make the process feel isolating. Finding ways to connect with like-minded individuals can significantly help address this difficulty.

An excessive focus on personal growth can lead to burnout if not balanced with rest and relaxation. It is important to find a healthy balance that allows for rejuvenation and a sense of well-being. There is the risk of falling into the trap of perfectionism or setting unrealistic expectations. This can lead to feeling you are striving for unattainable goals. It is important to develop reasonable expectations.

Personal growth can sometimes lead to comparing yourself to others and feeling inadequate or insecure. It is important to remember that personal growth is an individual journey. Each person's progress is unique. Focusing on your own growth rather than comparing yourself to others is important for maintaining a healthy mindset.

> *"Success is not final, failure is not fatal:*
> *it is the courage to continue that counts."*
> Winston Churchill

IMPORTANCE TO AN EMPLOYER

An employee who seeks personal growth has immense appeal to employers. Such individuals are driven by a commitment to self-improvement. This type of person will always contribute to a company's success and long-term growth because they are adaptable and open to new challenges.

They embrace change and more easily transition between tasks. Their agility proves invaluable in dynamic work environments where flexibility is vital, enabling the company to navigate market shifts and technological advancements with ease.

An employee committed to personal growth is likely to exhibit strong problem-solving skills. Their dedication to self-improvement fosters the development of critical thinking and analytical reasoning. These qualities enable them to approach challenges with a positive and strategic mindset.

Such employees often exhibit a strong commitment to their roles and the company's mission. Their continuous pursuit of excellence and advancement causes them to align with the organization's goals, fostering a sense of shared purpose and dedication. This positive work attribute boosts morale and enhances employee performance.[0]

EXAMPLES: Personal Growth Core Value Statements

1. I am committed to embracing learning as a lifelong activity.

2. My core value of personal growth drives me to continually learn, evolve, and expand my horizons.

3. I prioritize self-improvement, actively seeking opportunities to enhance my skills and knowledge.

4. I will embrace personal growth in order to overcome challenges and adapt to a changing world.

5. I believe that learning is the key to unlocking my full potential.

6. My commitment to personal growth fuels my resilience and ability to thrive in challenging circumstances.

7. I value the process of continuous learning and development both professionally and personally.

8. I approach life with a growth mindset, viewing every experience as an opportunity for learning and growth.

9. I am on a mission to elevate myself through personal growth, inspiring others to do the same.

MY PERSONAL CORE VALUE – Personal Growth

Adopt or confirm your core value. If personal growth is already a core value, or if you want to establish it as a core value, write your personal core value in the space below. You may want to use the examples above as guides to draft your Personal Core Value Statement. Make it short and meaningful to you. Something you can easily remember.

Personal Growth:

_____
_____
_____
_____
_____

DISCUSSION AND THOUGHT QUESTIONS

1. What does learning and personal growth mean to you? How would you personally define or describe it as a core value?

2. How important is personal growth as a core value? Why?

3. How has pursuing a mindset of learning and personal growth impacted your own life? Share specific examples.

4. What are some potential benefits and advantages of prioritizing personal growth as a core value in your life?

5. Reflecting on your own experiences, what challenges have you faced in pursuing personal growth? Did you overcome them?

6. How does personal growth contribute to one's overall well-being and personal fulfillment? In what ways does it positively impact various areas of life, such as family or career?

7. What is the connection between learning and adaptability? How does regular learning help in being more flexible?

8. What role does curiosity play for you in the pursuit of learning and personal growth? How does cultivating curiosity enhance your desire for increased knowledge?

9. How difficult do you find it to stay motivated to be continually learning? Can you relate any personal experience?

10. Discuss the role of mentors, role models, or influential individuals in fostering learning and personal growth.

NOTES

I want to do the following:

a. _____
b. _____
c. _____

I want to remember:

a. _____
b. _____
c. _____

Action Challenge: Identify a limiting belief that's holding you back from pursuing your goals. Challenge that belief by gathering evidence to the contrary and visualizing yourself succeeding despite it. Commit to taking one small step outside your comfort zone this week to foster personal growth.

Chapter 13
Diligence

DILIGENCE LIFE PRINCIPLE:
I will be diligent and hard-working.

*"There's nothing impossible
if you get up and work for it."*
Michael Flatley

IMPORTANT NOTE:
This chapter is a condensed version of our book *Choose Good Work Habits* in the Life Planning Series. The subject of diligence or working hard is included here in order to provide a more complete coverage of Core Values in this book. Diligence and your work ethic is a more complex subject than can be covered in this one chapter. For a more in-depth coverage of this subject, order a copy of *Choose Good Work Habits* [https://www.amazon.com/dp/1952359414].

GENERAL

We are covering three similar concepts in this chapter: being diligent, being a hard worker, and your work ethic. These are all habits designed to produce high quality outcomes. Remember that the core value of working hard is not just the practice of putting out a good effort, but also work that produces a good result. You should not be satisfied with working hard and achieving poor results.

Work has value

There are some obvious reasons why work has *intrinsic value*. First, if it serves others in some way, it benefits the needs of society. We must all work in order to provide for our own needs and those of our family. In addition, society is responsible for the poor and needy. The poor have always been with us, therefore, part of the responsibility of those capable of working is to help care for and provide for those who cannot work. Our attitude toward work should be consistent with the concept that our work matters and has value.

If your hope in life is to just get by with the least amount of effort, you will probably live a stressful and possibly miserable life. Rewards and success generally happen to those who are diligent, work hard, and achieve commendable results. Rewards are unlikely to be received by individuals looking for ways to avoid work.

Our work impacts the lives of our families, our employer, and anyone we might choose to help. It may be the quality and value of our work has more cumulative impact on others than it does on ourselves.

> *"A dream doesn't become reality through magic;*
> *it takes sweat, determination and hard work."*
> Colin Powell

Choose diligence

What is meant by the term diligence? A diligent person is considered to be steady, earnest, and committed. He is energetic, alert, and able to accomplish the task at hand. He is also devoted or committed to accomplishing the task. He will not give up.

If you have a good work ethic and diligence is a core value, you will be active and earnest in accomplishing the work you have undertaken. You will do the work today and not put it off until tomorrow. Finally you will take responsibility for what you do.

You choose to be diligent and it is in your best interest to generate a reputation as a hard worker. Diligence is much easier to accomplish if you are naturally energetic and industrious. If your work reputation is known and respected by others, you have significant advantages in your life. A reputation for diligence improves your ability to land good jobs and improve your position in life.

Everything you do is observed by others. When you work hard, do a job well, and exhibit diligence, others will observe you and your reputation will grow. Others are likely to seek your services and may even want your advice.

Those with a reputation for being lazy, idle, or apathetic do not have anyone seeking them out for work or any other opportunities.

Henry Ford said that you cannot build a reputation on what you are *going to do*. He means we must actually produce something other than talk. Promises only count if they are met. Empty promises will lead to a poor reputation. Establishing your work ethic will require being diligent, trustworthy, and ultimately producing high quality results. Talking about what you will do or can do won't impress anyone unless you deliver on your promises.

Being diligent can be described as being industrious. Diligent people are not idle but actively engaged in the work. They are busy and focused on accomplishing a given task.

Other terms that are often used to describe a good work ethic are reliability and dependability. Someone who is diligent will be earnest and committed to achieving a good result. The diligent worker is fully engaged and certainly not lazy.

> *"Things may come to those who wait,*
> *but only the things left by those who hustle."*
> Abraham Lincoln

Benefits of being diligent

There are many benefits for being a diligent worker. We have already mentioned several above. The following four benefits are also important.

- *You earn the respect of others.* Respect means that you are held in high regard and admired for your work ethic.

- *You have a good reputation because of your work ethic.* People will want to hire you. Having a good work ethic will produce a reputation that will be admired and sought out by others.

- *You feel good about yourself.* Feeling good about your work results in a high degree of self-confidence. A good self-image will allow you to accept more responsibility and undertake challenges that others with low self-esteem might shy away from. Diligence will lead to increased success in both your personal and professional life.

- *You will be considered for other opportunities*. A reputation for diligence and hard work often results in being offered other opportunities, projects, or jobs. These opportunities may be in areas other than your work or career because diligence is a universally desired trait.

> **"The first qualification for success in my view is a strong work ethic."**
> Henry Ford II

HARD WORK

The advice columnist Ann Landers said, "Nobody ever drowned in his own sweat." In other words, hard work is not going to kill you. Nothing is more desirable to a potential employer than individuals who work hard. Eric Thomas has said, "All roads that lead to success have to pass through hard work boulevard at some point."

Standing around

As a teenager, working for my best friend's older brother in the construction business, I quickly learned to identify workers who were there to work and those who just wanted a paycheck. When I was a kid helping my dad around the house, he would often tell me to open my eyes: "There is work right in front of you – don't let it bite you!" I usually heard this tender suggestion when I was standing around waiting to be told what to do.

That advice somehow sunk into my DNA because when I got my first real job I was aware of what was going on and what we were doing. So when the boss picked up a 2X4 to cut the end off I automatically grabbed the other end so that it was easier for him to cut.

It's one thing to stand around when you don't know what to do. It's another to ignore the obvious and be totally disengaged from your work. Remember, others are watching and aware of those who are engaged and those who are not.

If you want to see if someone is a good worker, watch what they do when they are working with others. Do they fade into the background or do they participate fully in accomplishing the task? Do they anticipate what needs to be done next, or do they need to be told? Do they assist without being asked? Do they make suggestions for how the job might be more easily accomplished?

Good work lasts, like quality appliances that do not break down in the first couple of years. My dad drilled into me that if I was going to do something, I should do it well. Why waste the time and effort if what you are doing is shoddy and unreliable? Nobody gains anything from mediocre work. Whatever you do, do it well!

> *"Nothing worthwhile comes easily.*
> *Work, continuous work, and hard work,*
> *is the only way to accomplish results that last."*
> Hamilton Holt

ATTITUDES TOWARD WORK

Unfortunately, some negative attitudes and habits have developed about work. Some feel that the objective in a job is to do as little as possible. This has led to several negative attitudes about work:

> *Who cares? I'm bored.* Many people are bored with their responsibilities, bored with the people they work with, and bored with life in general. They are bored, they are boring, and others resent their boredom. Nobody wants to work or be around these people.

> *Questionable ethics!* Your actions show who you really are and what you value. Issues of morality, ethics, and integrity confront us in every line of work. Are you cheating the person or company out of time, effort, or money while doing the job?

Steve Jobs took another view of work. He expected and demanded excellence. If you have ever worked in this type of situation, you know that the whole environment and approach to work is different. There is nothing wrong with having fun and taking breaks, but the purpose for breaks is rejuvenation. The work area atmosphere is geared to challenging everyone to do their very best, to find solutions to problems, not to entertain.

> *"Be a yardstick of quality. Some people aren't used to an environment where excellence is expected."*
> Steve Jobs

Workaholics

At the other end of the spectrum are people who believe that work determines self-worth. For these people work, career, and advancement are the core of life. Everything important revolves around work, power, success, and the level of compensation. Achievement on the job controls how they act and who they are. A successful career is the ultimate goal and all other areas of life such as family, health, and religion are subordinate to the career goal.

Over-involvement in a career has, historically, been a particular problem for *men.* Today, however, career-oriented women are lured into the same trap.

Workaholics may produce acceptable work but the demands on their personal life can be physically demanding on themselves and sometimes on those they work with. It is desirable to be passionate about your work, but it is not the most important aspect of life.

DO YOUR BEST

Regardless of the nature of the work, you should do the very best you can do. If you are cheating your employer on the time and effort you are giving to your job, you are actually cheating yourself. Good things come to people who deserve them. They earn them through good work, being diligent on the job, and going the extra mile. These characteristics will pay big dividends. Most organizations care a great deal about the quality of their products. If your work ethic is endangering the quality or the reputation of the company, you may find yourself looking for work someplace else.

In the matter of life and career we need to play the game better than our competitors and enemies. In the real world we compete with people who will not necessarily have our same values or perspectives. Wise people look at work the way it is, understand the nature of what they are doing, and do it the very best way they can. Their goal is excellence. They figure out the smart way to do things. They determine the best course of action and apply their skills to accomplish the task.

> *"Opportunities are usually disguised as hard work,*
> *so most people don't recognize them."*
> Ann Landers

Whether the work is for yourself or somebody else, it should be the best you can do. Nobody wants shoddy work. Here are several tips that will help you develop a good work ethic:

1. *Establish Core Values*. Establish personal core values for your work. Set standards of excellence.

2. *Employ Self-discipline*. Be a self-starter. Motivate yourself to work hard. Be intentional about the quality of your work.

3. *Be Flexible*. Be willing and able to adapt to new, changing, or different ways of doing things. Be open to change.

4. *Communicate Well*. Communicate clearly and openly to others about the work. Be positive and focus on solutions.

5. *Be Focused*. Eliminate distractions. Ignore what is unimportant.

6. *Maximize Your Strengths*. Work on weaknesses but don't undertake projects where your weaknesses must be strengths.

Diligence is rewarded in the workplace both verbally and monetarily. Good work and excellence will be recognized and often acclaimed by co-workers. Observers may even try to copy what you do and how you do it. Copying attitudes or good work practices is the greatest form of flattery.

Being industrious and working hard produces a result that you can be proud of. This leads to greater self-confidence and ultimately better results. You set a good example for others.

> **"Talent is never enough. With few exceptions
> the best players are the hardest workers."**
> Magic Johnson

KEYS TO BEING DILIGENT

Be consistent. Working hard is important but life and work are not sprints: they are marathons. In addition to working hard we also need to work regularly and consistently. It is much better to be there every day than to exhaust your mind and body with frequent fifteen-hour days. Don't overwork yourself on one day so the next day is a blur.

Be focused. If you are easily distracted, it is difficult to produce quality work. Your heart and mind must be focused on the task at hand, not thinking about sports, dates, hobbies, etc.

Be positive. In general, positive attitudes in all areas of life will be beneficial. If you have a positive outlook on life, problems seem to have a different impact than if you are always grumbling and complaining about your circumstances. Negative attitudes have a significant impact on your work performance. Practice positive self-talk, if necessary. Focus on successes, not failures. Don't let mistakes, difficulties, or setbacks get you down. Both work and life will have ups and downs. Encourage others with your positive attitude.

Be yourself. Finally, know your skills, abilities, and strengths as well as your weaknesses. Work to your strengths and minimize your weaknesses. Don't undertake an important job or project that will depend on being good at something you don't like or can't do well.

> **"The dictionary is the only place that success comes
> before work. Work is the key to success, and hard
> work can help you accomplish anything."**
> Vince Lombardi

THE BENEFITS OF HARD WORK

Growth. Hard work leads to self-development and improvement. No matter our age, health, or status, we should be actively pursuing self-improvement.

Confidence. Hard work, diligence, and striving for excellence helps build confidence in our abilities.

Compensation. Hard work produces higher compensation and allows us to enjoy the benefits that come with a higher income. Our work can allow us to be generous and benefit others, particularly the needy.

Attitude. Working hard establishes a foundation for gratitude and other important core values. When we are upbeat and grateful for what we have, life is easier. Grumbling and whining make life difficult.

Achievement. Accomplishments bring a sense of achievement and satisfaction. Opportunities for leadership are often made available to high achievers. Results allow you to be seen and heard while others never get that chance. Diligence and hard work will keep you ahead of the competition. Your work ethic can attract meaningful opportunities, both personal and professional.

Reputation and Respect. Diligence and hard work command respect. Even those who do not want to work usually respect the diligent worker. Those with less drive and commitment may not particularly like you, but they will respect your work ethic.

Friends. People love to make friends with those who have a good work ethic. You will also tend to be less stressed if you have friends who support you in difficult times. Friends can be a great encouragement when problems happen. They can help you overcome the roadblocks that life puts in your path.

Less Stress. Diligence means you never have to be ashamed of your work or what you have produced. Hard work and diligence create a sense of accomplishment, enriching your life as well as reducing stress

Legacy. Through diligence you can leave behind a meaningful legacy inspired by a culture of hard work and dedication. Results produced by hard work are deeply satisfying and can influence others to perform well. Your example can leave a lasting legacy. Being a role model for hard work and diligence can have a lasting influence on family, co-workers, and even your community.

I WAS JUST CHECKING

A young man rushed into a service station one day and asked the manager if he had a pay phone. The manager nodded, "Sure, over there." The guy inserted a couple of coins, dialed and waited for an answer. Finally someone came on the line. "Uh, sir," he said in a deep voice, "could you use an honest, hard-working young man?" The service station manager couldn't help overhearing the question. After a moment the young man said, "Oh, you already have an honest, hard-working young man? Well, okay. Thanks all the same."

A broad smile stretched across his face. He hung up the phone and started back to his car, obviously elated. "Hey, just a minute," the station manager said, "I couldn't help but hear your conversation. Why are you so happy? I thought the man said he already had someone and didn't need you?" The young man smiled, "Well, you see, I am that honest, hard-working young man. I was just checking up on myself!"[4]

Checking up on yourself is really good advice. Maybe it should not be done under the circumstances described in this story, but the concept is valid. How are you doing? If you are on a path of self-improvement, trying to be the best you can be, are you making progress? Successful people want to know how they are doing in order to take corrective action, if necessary.

Ask your boss. Ask your coworkers. Ask your friends. Ask your spouse. Examine the results you are producing. Is there evidence of change? If not, what do you need to do? Are there any problems you need to correct in order to do a better job? Do you need more knowledge and understanding to do a job well? Or do you just need time?

If you have difficulty with self-examination, have someone who knows you well do it with you. If you choose this alternative, be very selective in your choice. Don't do this if you are not mature enough to hear and receive constructive criticism.

> *The difference between being concerned and*
> *being committed is that when you're committed,*
> *you accept no excuses, only results.*

PRACTICAL TIPS

Here are a number of easy-to-implement tips for developing or practicing the personal core value of diligence:

1. Have achievable goals for yourself. Stay focused.

2. Establish a routine that includes dedicated time for the most important tasks and responsibilities. Use task management tools to prioritize tasks based on importance and deadlines.

3. Divide larger tasks into smaller, more manageable steps.

4. Minimize interruptions by turning off your phone or creating a quiet workspace environment.

5. Keep both physical and digital spaces organized.

6. Start tasks promptly, even when you don't feel like it.

7. Invite constructive criticism from peers or mentors.

IMPORTANCE TO AN EMPLOYER

An employee who is diligent and has a strong work ethic is a prized asset in any organization. Such qualities bring numerous benefits that contribute to the success of both the employee and the company.

First and foremost, employees with diligence and a commitment to hard work will consistently strive for excellence. They take ownership of their responsibilities, ensuring that every project is completed well.

Diligence-driven employees are reliable. They meet deadlines, fulfill commitments, and consistently deliver good results. This reliability instills confidence in colleagues and clients, fostering strong relationships and effective collaboration. When co-workers know they can count on someone to consistently contribute their best effort, teamwork becomes more efficient and productive.

Such employees are more likely to exhibit perseverance in the face of challenges. They don't shy away from hard work. They approach challenges with determination and a desire to find workable solutions. This contributes to improved problem-solving and better results.

The dedication of diligent employees often extends beyond their own responsibilities. They step up to assist team members and offer support. Their willingness to help creates a supportive environment that encourages others to raise their own level of commitment.[0]

"Plan your work for today and every day, then work your plan."
Margaret Thatcher

EXAMPLES: Diligence Core Value Statements

Here are some sample core value statements you might choose if you were adopting diligence and hard work as your personal core value:

1. I value diligence and hard work. I commit to consistently give my best effort in all tasks and endeavors.

2. I prioritize diligence, approaching each task with unwavering dedication to achieve excellence.

3. Diligence is at the heart of my core values, driving me to persevere and overcome challenges with determination.

4. I embrace hard work as a fundamental principle, continuously seeking improvement in my performance.

5. I am dedicated to hard work and diligence.

6. I believe in the power of hard work to transform obstacles into stepping stones to outstanding performance.

7. I am steadfast in my pursuit of doing my best.

8. Hard work is my compass, guiding me to approach each task with a sense of purpose and dedication.

9. I choose to embrace hard work as a cornerstone of my personal character.

10. I am driven by the principle that consistent effort and hard work are essential for personal and collective success.

> *"The best way to learn is by doing. The only way to build a strong work ethic is getting your hands dirty."*
> Alex Spanos

MY PERSONAL CORE VALUE – Diligence and Hard Work

Adopt or confirm your core value. If diligence and hard work are already core values, or if you want to establish them in your life, write your personal core value in the space below. You may want to use the examples above as guides to draft your Personal Core Value Statement. Make it short, succinct, and meaningful to you. Something you can easily remember.

Diligence and Hard Work:

_____

_____

_____

_____

_____

_____

_____

DISCUSSION AND THOUGHT QUESTIONS

1. What does diligence mean to you and why is it important in your personal life or work environment?

2. How do you measure your own performance when evaluating whether you are diligent?

3. What are the benefits of working hard and being diligent?

4. What are some of the challenges or obstacles that prevent you from being diligent or working hard?

5. How do you balance your work and personal life without compromising the quality of your work?

6. How do you motivate yourself to work hard and be diligent?

7. How do you handle feedback or criticism about your work? Do you encourage feedback?

8. How do you learn from your mistakes or failures in your work?

9. How do you collaborate with others who have different work ethics or expectations?

10. How do you deal with stress or burnout in your work?

"The difference between the impossible and the possible lies in a man's determination."
Tommy Lasorda

NOTES: I want to do or remember:

a. _____
b. _____
c. _____
d. _____
e. _____

Action Challenge: Identify a long-term goal you've been struggling to achieve. Break it down into smaller, manageable tasks and create a daily schedule that prioritizes those tasks. Commit to following this schedule diligently for one week, tracking your progress and celebrating small victories along the way.

Chapter 14
Honor and Respect
RESPECT LIFE PRINCIPLE:
I will honor others and my core values.

"Respect is earned. Honesty is appreciated.
Trust is gained. Loyalty is returned."
Unknown

GENERAL

The core values of honor and respect encompass a deep sense of dignity and regard for yourself and others.

Honor, as a personal core value, implies living in alignment with a strong moral and ethical foundation. It involves conducting yourself with honesty and a commitment to upholding your principles and values, even in the face of challenges or temptations.

Respect involves recognizing the inherent worth and rights of others. It includes valuing diverse perspectives and treating others with kindness, fairness, and equality. Respect for yourself means having good self-esteem and setting healthy boundaries.

The combination of honor and respect as personal core values creates a foundation for positive relationships and effective communication. When you honor and respect others you help create an environment in which people feel valued. This will enable you to build meaningful relationships with others.

"Respect is a two-way street.
If you want to get it, you've got to give it."
R.G. Risch

NATURE OF HONOR AND RESPECT

Those committed to honor and respect will draw upon numerous other principles and character traits. Here are some of the other personal attributes that come into play when embracing respect and honor as a core value:

Integrity
Acting with honesty and upholding ethical principles will be a fundamental part of your character when honor is a core value. You will honor commitments, be true to your word, and maintain consistency between your words and actions.

Trust
If you value honor and respect, trustworthiness will be an element in your relationships. By treating people with fairness and dignity you create an environment in which trust is a foundational character trait. Others will feel valued and comfortable, leading to a sense of belonging within the family unit or work group.

Honorable behavior will always promote a sense of moral responsibility and help individuals navigate ethical dilemmas. Individuals who consistently demonstrate high ethical values earn the trust of others. This fosters effective teamwork and leadership based on similar underlying principles that honor one another.

Relationships
Embracing honor and respect builds positive and meaningful relationships. It produces open communication which results in deeper connections and a sense of mutual support. Honor and respect also contribute to self-confidence and a positive self-image. Prioritizing these values builds trust and leads to more open and honest interaction with others. Respect will strengthen personal bonds and deepen connections which ultimately produce strong and long-lasting relationships.

Conflict Resolution
Honor and respect inherently equip you with skills for more easily resolving conflicts. Your ability to find common ground will lead to workable resolutions and improved outcomes.

You will respect personal boundaries, both physical and emotional. Aggressive words or behavior, no matter how strongly your beliefs, will never create space for understanding or agreement.

Respect is always the best foundation for effective conflict resolution. When people approach conflicts with respect and a willingness to understand different perspectives, disagreements are more easily resolved. The skill of active and effective listening while being conscious of diverse or different opinions will normally lead to more positive outcomes. It is simply much easier to find workable solutions in an atmosphere of trust and respect.

Equality

Individuals who value others and treat them with respect will contribute to a more friendly, inclusive, and equitable group or community. By recognizing the dignity of every individual, differences can be bridged and real results accomplished.

Honor and respect encourage inclusivity and equality. They allow the participation of individuals from different backgrounds and experiences to come together on common ground. They produce social harmony among diverse groups and promote cooperative interaction. These values create a ripple effect of positive change. Common core values provide a platform for common understanding and open the door for inspiring others to embrace those same values.

Those who value equality speak up against discrimination, prejudice, and injustice, both within personal circles and in the broader community. Remaining silent is often interpreted as favoring discrimination. Do not hesitate to speak up, but do it with respect.

Dignity

Treating every individual with dignity, regardless of their background or position is a must. Listen carefully to the opinions of others and engage them in meaningful discussions (not arguments). Courtesy should guide all of your interactions.

Communication

Engage in respectful communication, always using tact and constructive language. Avoid offensive remarks! No one will respect you if you treat others rudely. If you disagree with an opinion, try asking questions until it becomes obvious which opinion holds the most merit.

Summary

Those who act with honor and respect will have a sense of purpose and fulfillment, in addition to a deeper connection to others. You can serve as a role model for others, particularly children and younger generations. By demonstrating these values, you will inspire others to follow suit.

CHALLENGES

The decision to act with honor and respect can present certain difficulties and challenges.

First, cultural and personal biases can be challenging. These biases influence your perception of others and hinder your ability to treat everyone equally. Recognizing and addressing prejudice requires self-awareness and a willingness to challenge your assumptions and feelings. We all have our own cultural bias.

Second, be aware of possible emotional triggers. Emotions can cloud our judgment and lead to reactive behavior. Managing emotions can be challenging, especially in heated or stressful situations. Being in control is essential to being respectful and treating others honorably.

Third, peer pressure and social norms can sometimes undermine efforts to act honorably. Conforming to negative norms or engaging in disrespectful acts in order to fit in can be tempting. Resisting these pressures and staying true to your values requires courage and a strong sense of personal integrity. Language barriers, differences in communication styles, or cultural habits can hinder effective interaction and understanding.

Conflict resolution can be challenging when emotions run high or when there are deeply rooted differences. Finding mutually agreeable solutions that respect all parties involved requires patience. Effective and open communication is often the key to conflict resolution.

> *"Respect is not something you demand, it's something you earn."*
> Unknown

CONSEQUENCES

Disrespect can have significant negative consequences. Here are some of the potential difficulties that can occur when you fail to act honorably or treat others with respect.

Relationships. Lack of respect for others' opinions, boundaries, or feelings will strain relationships. When individuals demonstrate a lack of respect, others will not want to be around them or work with them.

In professional settings the absence of respect will hinder career growth. Employers hesitate to provide opportunities to individuals who do not treat others with dignity.

Lack of respect in a family can strain relationships and produce dysfunction. Ignoring the boundaries of others will produce ongoing conflicts and fractured family bonds that can last a long time.

Reputation. Being disrespectful to others will result in a negative reputation. This will affect how you are perceived by others in personal, professional, and community settings. Negative reputations limit opportunities and hinder personal growth. In work environments the absence of respect can destroy teamwork, and create a toxic atmosphere in which communication breaks down, conflicts escalate, and productivity suffers.

Isolation. Individuals who disrespect others may find themselves isolated or excluded from social circles. People naturally gravitate towards those who treat them well and honor their feelings and boundaries. The absence of friends can lead to feelings of loneliness and can impact an individual's emotional and mental well-being.

Legal and Ethical Consequences. The lack of respect can sometimes lead to unethical or illegal behaviors. Disregard for others' rights can result in legal consequences and have long-term negative impact on both personal and professional life.

> *"Honor is what keeps a man upright,*
> *even when others falter."*
> Unknown

IMPORTANCE TO AN EMPLOYER

An employee who embodies the core values of respect and honor is very valuable to any organization. These attributes contribute significantly to a positive work environment and effective teamwork. Employees who exhibit respect establish a foundation of trust within the organization. Their genuine consideration for colleagues fosters open communication and enhances working relationships. This leads to reduced conflicts and a more productive workplace.

Individuals with these core values generally have high ethical standards. Their commitment to doing what is right, even when no one is watching, enhances the organization's reputation and credibility. Employers can rely on these employees to make principled decisions consistent with the company's own core values.

Those who embody respect are usually adept at conflict resolution. They approach conflict with a willingness to understand different perspectives. This skill significantly reduces workplace tension and enables more effective problem-solving.

Such employees also tend to be more patient and resilient. They approach change with an open mind and are more likely to support company transitions. This flexibility enhances the organization's ability to thrive in a dynamic business environment.

Honor and respect are also closely connected to career advancement because they build strong relationships in the workplace. They are necessary for effective leaders. Colleagues, managers, and clients will admire workers who consistently demonstrate respect for others.[0]

Respect for yourself guides character!

EXAMPLES: Respect and Honor Core Value Statements

1. I value and prioritize treating every individual with respect.

2. Honor will guide my actions, decisions, and relationships.

3. My core values are centered on demonstrating respect and honor in all aspects of my life.

4. I commit to upholding a culture of respect and honor, both in my personal and professional life.

5. I believe in the power of respect and honor to create positive relationships and foster personal connections.

6. I am dedicated to practicing respect and honor as foundational principles in my everyday life.

7. I am unwavering in my commitment to treating everyone with honor and respect.

8. I hold true to the principles of respect and honor, aiming to inspire and influence those around me to do the same.

MY PERSONAL CORE VALUE – Respect and Honor

Adopt or confirm your core value. If respect and honor are already a core value, or if you want to establish it as a core value, write your personal core value in the space below. You may want to use the examples above as guides to draft your Personal Core Value Statement. Make it short, succinct, and meaningful to you. Something you can easily remember.

Respect and Honor:

_____
_____
_____
_____
_____
_____
_____
_____

DISCUSSION AND THOUGHT QUESTIONS

1. What does respect mean to you? How would you define it?

2. Think of a time when you felt disrespected or dishonored. How did it affect you and your relationships with others?

3. What are some practical ways in which we can demonstrate respect and honor towards others in personal interactions?

4. How do respect and honor contribute to building and healthy relationships, both personal and professional?

5. In what ways do you think respect influences teamwork?

6. How do respect and honor foster a sense of belonging or inclusivity in a community or organization?

7. Can you share an example of a public or historical figure who exemplifies the values of respect and honor? Describe.

8. Do respect and honor influence decision-making? Why?

9. What role do you think respect plays in conflict resolution?

10. How can we cultivate a culture of respect within our families and schools? What could you do to promote respect in these areas?

NOTES: I want to do or remember the following:

a. _____
b. _____
c. _____
d. _____
e. _____
f. _____
g. _____

Action Challenge: Reflect on how well you treat yourself and others. Identify one area where you can improve your self-respect or show greater respect for others. Commit to making that change this week, whether it's practicing self-care, setting boundaries, or actively listening to someone else's perspective.

Chapter 15
Justice
and Fairness

JUSTICE LIFE PRINCIPLE:
I will do what is right and fair.

"Justice cannot be for one side alone,
but must be for both."
Eleanor Roosevelt

INTRODUCTION

The personal core value of justice is a fundamental principle that should constantly guide individuals in their interactions with others. It reflects a commitment to treating people right.

Justice is the pursuit of what is right. It involves upholding moral principles, ensuring that individuals are treated equitably. It includes the concept of accountability and holding individuals responsible for their decisions and actions.

Fairness, on the other hand, encompasses the concept of treating people "equally" regardless of their background, status, or personal attributes. It involves being objective and unbiased in the decision-making process. Fairness requires the absence of discrimination and favoritism, promoting equal opportunities for all.

Together, these core values form a powerful combination that promotes ethical behavior and creates social harmony. They encourage the stand against inequality, oppression, and injustice.

"Injustice anywhere is a threat
to justice everywhere."
Martin Luther King Jr.

ASPECTS OF JUSTICE

Justice inherently requires equitable treatment for everyone. It means making impartial decisions. This core value is rooted in ethical and righteous principles. It calls for acting in accordance with morally correct values and principles. It requires an attitude or desire for equitable treatment of all people. Justice inherently aligns with the rule of law and emphasizes the importance of a just legal system.

True justice advocates for societal changes that promote fairness and equality. Such perspectives can become closely tied to the protection and respect for human rights.

The desire for social justice will generally produce a strong desire for restoration. Those seeking peaceful, fair, and inclusive solutions to conflicts will tend to become involved in advocacy and activism to address social injustices.

Justice and fairness also imply holding individuals and institutions accountable for their actions. It includes taking responsibility for actions and encouraging others to do the same.

> *"Justice is not about bringing people down,*
> *it's about lifting people up."*
> Condoleezza Rice

THE SIGNIFICANCE

The personal core value of justice can hold significant influence in all aspects of life. It impacts family life, influencing relationships, decision-making, and even overall well-being. It can impact relationships both within the family and the workplace, prompting communication and enhancing resolution in all relationships.

When people approach disagreements with a commitment to justice and fairness, they seek equitable solutions that consider the needs and perspectives of everyone involved. This allows harmony to be maintained while seeking reconciliation.

Justice and fairness are both important for parents in raising a family. By treating children justly and fairly, parents instill important values of equality and respect, creating a foundation for children to grow into compassionate individuals. Children who are treated unfairly will treat others unfairly. Through discussions and leading by example, parents can help children understand the importance of justice and fairness in their interactions with others.

When family members or friends are confident that they will be treated fairly and justly, an environment in which individuals feel safe and valued is created. It is important in both the family and workplace to exhibit trust and transparency. Work and chores within the family unit need not be divided equally because of the age and capabilities of the children, but they should not be perceived as unfair.

Overall, the personal core value of justice and fairness brings immense significance to personal and family life by fostering healthy relationships. It shapes the family dynamics and prepares individuals to extend justice to the broader environment around them.

"Justice is truth in action."
Benjamin Disraeli

DEMONSTRATING JUSTICE

Demonstrating justice requires intentional actions and behaviors that uphold righteousness, honesty, and ethical conduct. We have mentioned some of these above. Following is a list of eight common practices in which you can demonstrate justice or fairness:

1. Treating others equally, with respect and dignity.

2. Actively listening to the perspectives and opinions of others.

3. Making decisions based on impartiality – avoiding favoritism.

4. Standing up against discrimination or inequality.

5. Seeking fair and constructive resolutions based on the concerns of everyone involved.

6. Challenging your own biases and the biases of others.

7. Practicing justice and fairness in your personal conversations, public communications, and actions.

8. Mentoring and educating others, especially younger people.

WHY IMPORTANT?

Why are the core values of justice and fairness important? The first and perhaps most obvious reason is that justice and fairness are fundamental to upholding and safeguarding human rights which impact the entire society. Just people contribute to creating a society in which every person is treated with dignity and respect.

Justice and fairness ensure that everyone has equal opportunities to succeed and thrive, regardless of their socio-economic status, gender, race, or other personal characteristics. This value is essential for breaking down inequitable barriers that exist in society.

Justice and fairness are foundational to building trust and confidence among individuals and institutions. When people know that they will be treated right, it strengthens their faith in the value of systems and promotes cooperation. Leaders who prioritize these values inspire trust and loyalty.

Justice and fairness also encourage compassion toward others. Individuals who value these principles are more likely to understand the struggles and challenges faced by others. This leads to increased empathy and understanding. Knowing about the issues and difficulties of others makes it easier to recognize and address systemic inequalities and advocate for policies that help the marginalized or disadvantaged.

> *"Fairness is not an attitude. It's a professional skill that must be developed and exercised."*
> Brit Hume

CHALLENGES

Implementing the personal core values of justice and fairness brings its own set of challenges. This may be more difficult than other commitments you might undertake.

Overcoming your own internal biases is challenging. Recognizing and addressing deeply ingrained beliefs or prejudices requires self-confidence, humility, and a willingness to confront uncomfortable truths about yourself. This can be a significant challenge for anyone!

In addition, issues involving justice and fairness are often complex. Understanding the root causes of systemic inequalities and navigating the complexities of social issues can be overwhelmingly difficult. It may require actively seeking expert help.

Engaging with topics related to justice can evoke strong emotions. Confronting the injustices and inequities present in society can be emotionally challenging. This can lead to feelings of anger, frustration, or helplessness. Learning to manage these emotions constructively is crucial. Overcoming resistance and finding effective ways to communicate and persuade others can be a significant challenge because others have their own biases.

Promoting justice and fairness is often a long-term endeavor, requiring patience, perseverance, and recognition that meaningful change takes time. Slow progress and setbacks can be disheartening.

Addressing justice and fairness often involves coming face-to-face with the existing power structure in various environments. Navigating these dynamics while challenging existing power imbalances can be a complex and sometimes dangerous endeavor, especially if you are creating waves or disruption to someone's power base.

> *"A society can be judged by*
> *how it treats its weakest members."*
> Mahatma Gandhi

CONSEQUENCES

Without a fundamental commitment to justice, relationships can become strained or damaged. Unfair treatment, inequality, and disregard for the rights and perspectives of others can erode trust, leading to broken relationships and even retaliation.

The absence of justice perpetuates inequality and discrimination. When justice is absent, social conflict and unrest can arise. Families, organizations, and communities can become divided. Businesses and governments suffer significant losses and breakdowns when people lose faith in the integrity of an organization.

Without a commitment to justice and fairness, individuals and organizations may engage in unethical behavior, exploiting others for their personal gain. This can lead to a culture of corruption and dishonesty. Without justice an individual or organization can lose sight of their moral compass and act solely in their self-interest. This can lead to a disregard for the welfare and rights of others.

> *"Where justice is denied, where poverty is enforced, where ignorance prevails, neither persons nor property will be safe."*
> Frederick Douglass

PRACTICAL TIPS

Implementing justice and fairness as core values involves intentional actions and continual diligence. Here are some very practical tips and suggestions that can help you implement this core value:

1. Educate yourself about inequalities and injustices.

2. Challenge your own prejudices. Be open to recognizing and addressing inherent biases that may influence your actions.

3. Seek out diverse perspectives and actively listen to others' experiences and viewpoints.

4. Express your concerns when you witness injustice.

5. Contribute your time to organizations that promote justice.

6. Avoid making assumptions based on stereotypes.

7. Share information and stories that shed light on injustices that will inspire positive change.

8. Stand by those who face discrimination or injustice, offering your support.

IMPORTANCE TO AN EMPLOYER

An employee with the core value of justice brings a highly desirable set of qualities and principles to the workplace. Actions characterized by fairness, equality, and a commitment to doing what is right will have a profound impact on the workplace environment and contribute to the success of an organization.

An employee with a strong sense of justice is likely to treat colleagues and subordinates equitably, creating an atmosphere of trust and respect. This contributes to a positive work environment. In which employees feel valued and appreciated regardless of their background or personal characteristics. This sense of fairness will boost employee morale, motivation, and loyalty to the organization.

Employees with a strong sense of justice tend to uphold other high ethical standards. They are less likely to engage in unethical behavior and are more likely to hold themselves and their colleagues accountable for their actions. This contributes to a culture of integrity and accountability which is highly valued by employers seeking to build strong relationships with clients.

In decision-making processes, employees who prioritize justice will carefully consider the implications of their choices. Their ability to assess situations objectively, taking into account the needs and perspectives of different camps, leads to a more well-rounded and thoughtful decision. This will mitigate potential conflicts and promote a sense of confidence in the company and its leadership.

Employees who embody the value of justice often demonstrate exceptional leadership qualities. They are more likely to step forward as advocates for change and take on the responsibility of addressing workplace inequalities. This willingness to stand up for what is right will inspire others to act in a similar fashion.[0]

> *"Justice is the constant and perpetual*
> *will to allot to every man his due."*
> Domitus Ulpianus

EXAMPLES: Justice and Fairness Core Value Statements

1. I am committed to upholding fairness and equality in all my interactions and decisions.

2. Justice guides my actions, pushing me to stand up against discrimination and injustice wherever I encounter it.

3. My core value of justice motivates me to support the rights of the marginalized and underrepresented.

4. Upholding justice means recognizing and addressing my own biases to ensure impartiality in all I do.

5. My commitment to justice leads me to challenge practices that perpetuate unfair treatment of others.

6. I view justice as a guiding principle that shapes all my interactions and decisions.

7. I prioritize fairness and honesty in my endeavors, striving to be a role model for equitable behavior.

8. I value the principles of fairness and justice in both my personal life and professional career.

9. I believe in equitable systems, policies, and practices that treat everyone with fairness and justice.

MY PERSONAL CORE VALUE – Justice and Fairness

Adopt or confirm your core value. If justice is already a core value, or if you want to establish it as a core value, write your personal core value in the space below. You may want to use the examples above as guides to draft your Personal Core Value Statement. Make it short, succinct, and meaningful to you. Something you can easily remember.

Justice and Fairness:

_____
_____
_____
_____
_____
_____
_____
_____

DISCUSSION AND THOUGHT QUESTIONS

1. What does justice mean to you and how do you think it differs from fairness?

2. Why are justice and fairness important core values?

3. Share an experience in which you witnessed or experienced injustice. How did it make you feel, and how did you respond?

4. In your opinion, how does practicing justice contribute to a healthier and more inclusive community or workplace?

5. Why is it necessary to challenge and address your own biases and prejudices when striving for justice?

6. How can you use your voice and influence to raise awareness about injustices and inspire positive change in your area of influence?

7. Can justice and fairness coexist with individual rights and freedoms? How do you balance these values?

8. How does justice and fairness impact the concept of leadership? What are the responsibilities of leaders in promoting these values?

9. Can justice be achieved without a system of laws and regulations? What is the role of legal frameworks in upholding these values?

NOTES

I want to do the following:

a. _____
b. _____
c. _____
d. _____

I want to remember:

a. _____
b. _____
c. _____
d. _____

Action Challenge: Consider a situation where you witnessed an injustice. How did you respond? What could you have done differently to promote fairness and healing? Research local organizations working for justice and explore ways you can get involved in creating a more equitable society.

Chapter 16
Positive Attitudes

ATTITUDE LIFE PRINCIPLE:
I will have a positive attitude.

"Virtually nothing is impossible in this world
if you just put your mind to it and
maintain a positive attitude."
Lou Holtz

Special Note to Reader:
We are including this last chapter on positive attitudes because we believe having an uplifting attitude is a very valuable personal attribute. Thus, we are going to arbitrarily treat positive attitudes like a core value, but in reality it does not fall into the definition of a core value like all the others discussed in this book.

There are obviously a number of attitudes that impact one's life. Our focus in this chapter is on positive attitudes that will raise the spirit or performance of both the person in question and those around him. We have chosen eight such attitudes.

INTRODUCTION

We begin our discussion of attitudes with some advice from Mahatma Gandhi:

"Keep your thoughts positive because your thoughts become your words, words become your behavior, behavior becomes your habits, habits become your values, and your values become your destiny."

Gandhi is speaking about thoughts and attitudes that manifest themselves into words and acts that become personal habits and values. He says these attitudes will determine your destiny. He is absolutely right, but it is very difficult for most people to conceive how their thoughts and attitudes at age 25 are somehow going to determine the course of their life. But that is exactly what our thoughts and attitudes can do.

Lysa Terkeurst in her book, *The Best Yes,* says something very similar: "The decision you make determines the schedule you keep. The schedule you keep determines the life you live. And how you live your life determines how you spend your soul."[5]

Importance of attitudes

The fundamental message in these quotes is that your attitude can make a huge difference in your life. Gandhi says it will determine your destiny and Terkeurst says it will determine how you spend your soul.

I'm sure we could find a number of official definitions for attitude, but for our purposes we will think of it as a state of mind. It is how you generally respond to something. It is your mental position, feeling, or emotion in regard to something. It can be either positive or negative.

Our purpose in this chapter is to encourage you to develop positive or "uplifting" attitudes. By this we mean that your automatic response to life is positive, upbeat, and intended to influence others for the better. Your attitude should boost the spirits of others, elevate the conversation, or raise the quality of action or speech. A positive attitude can cause others to think, speak, and act better.

> *"The greatest day in your life and mine is when*
> *we take total responsibility for our attitudes.*
> *That's the day we truly grow up."*
> John C. Maxwell

Positive attitudes

Having positive attitudes can help you reduce stress, improve health, increase creativity, raise productivity, find solutions, improve relationships, increase happiness, and create a fulfilled life. That's a lot of positive results! Developing these attitudes takes time and practice but they will contribute significantly to living a more productive and meaningful life.

We are not going to discuss any of the attitudes in great depth. We only will provide a brief description since they are well-known and self-explanatory. Our goal is implementation, not explanation.

> *"The only disability in life*
> *is a bad attitude."*
> Scott Hamilton

OPTIMISM

The attitude of *optimism* refers to maintaining a positive outlook, expecting favorable outcomes, or emphasizing the hopeful aspects of a situation. It also involves perceiving challenges as opportunities for growth, believing in the potential for success, and approaching life or problems with confidence. Optimism fosters a sense of hope and well-being and influences how you respond to life.

Optimistic people look on the bright side of things and have a positive outlook for the future. Projecting optimism during difficult times will often inspire others to be more positive. It is very difficult for people with negative attitudes to inspire anyone else.

Optimism is frequently accompanied by confidence and self-assurance. It expects the best possible outcome and is focused on the positive aspects of a situation. Thus, it is easier to cope with stress and the challenges of the day.

ENCOURAGEMENT

Encouragement is the characteristic of giving someone support or hope. It refers to providing positive reinforcement to others. It includes recognizing or acknowledging the efforts of others. The encourager offers kind words, praise, and support.

Encouragement comes from many sources, such as family, friends, teachers, mentors, coaches, or other role models. It can be expressed in different ways, such as words, gestures, actions, gifts, or rewards. Encouragement will build confidence in yourself and others. Being an encourager can have a profound impact on others, inspiring them to believe in themselves and overcome difficult challenges.

OPEN-MINDEDNESS

Open-mindedness refers to a receptive and non-judgmental approach towards new ideas and experiences. It involves a willingness to consider alternative viewpoints and different possibilities. Open-minded people possess a genuine curiosity about the world, seeking to broaden their understanding. They are willing to challenge their own preconceived notions. This can be a refreshing attitude for the associates of such people.

Open-minded people are often more receptive and non-judgmental towards innovation. They are willing to consider alternative viewpoints and challenge their own beliefs. Such people approach problems with curiosity and a willingness to learn and grow. They are not locked into one way of doing things.

The open-minded person tends to be *proactive*. Being proactive means taking initiative and assuming responsibility for one's actions. Proactive individuals anticipate and actively seek out opportunities rather than wait for things to happen. They are driven by a sense of purpose and actively work toward achieving their goals. This characteristic is often the result of being open-minded.

ADAPTABILITY (flexibility)

Adaptability refers to the ability to adjust in response to new situations. It involves being flexible and willing to embrace change. Adaptable individuals demonstrate resourcefulness in navigating through uncertainty and rapidly changing circumstances. This characteristic is critical in a world of innovation and rapid technological advances.

Because adaptable individuals are not overwhelmed by change, they tend to think "outside the box" and explore new possibilities. They adapt their thinking and embrace emerging trends, leading to innovative ideas and solutions.

CURIOSITY

Curiosity can help you expand your knowledge, skills, and interests. You do this by trying new things and exploring different perspectives. Curiosity means you have a strong desire to learn about new things. You enjoy having new experiences.

Curiosity involves a sense of wonder resulting in a state of constant exploration driven by an inner inquisitiveness. Curious people have a willingness to delve deeper into subjects. They are driven to engage with the world around them while looking for new perspectives. They enjoy expanding their knowledge.

Curious people are very valuable in a time of innovation because their interest in new things and concepts produce ideas and solutions not considered by others.

HUMOR

The characteristic of being *humorous* is the ability to find humor in situations. It brings joy and amusement to oneself and to others. It involves a light-hearted approach to life, the use of wit, and the skill of finding something comedic in mundane situations. Being humorous can influence social interactions and improve relationships. It can also diffuse tense situations.

Having a sense of humor and being able to laugh at yourself can help you cope with stress and lighten the mood of those around you. It allows you to bond more easily with others simply because you are fun to be around.

ENTHUSIASM

Being *enthusiastic* about what you do can help you enjoy your work. It can motivate you to act and help achieve your goals. People who are inspired toward common goals by passionate leaders will generally produce better results. Such people tend to be more committed to their work.

The director of a stage play who exhibits little passion for the performance, shouldn't expect his actors to be any different. Followers imitate the attitudes of their leaders. Those who want to lead or engage others must be inspiring and passionate about what they are doing. Passion can be contagious to the point that followers will have the same level pf enthusiasm.

Being enthusiastic means having a genuine and often contagious passion, combined with positive energy, towards goals. It will often involve displaying eagerness and a proactive approach to embracing new challenges or experiences.

EXCELLENCE (doing your best)

Do your best. It will directly impact your life!
Do your best. Shoddy work will come back to haunt you.
Do your best. Somebody important may be watching you.
Do your best. You will have to live with the result.
Do your best. You will be judged on the result.
Do your best. Your job may depend on it.
Do your best. Your next-to-best will not be good enough.
Do your best. Your future may depend on it.

The underlying message here is that doing shoddy work, for whatever reason, produces nothing good. It could result in a loss of respect or reputation. It might even cause a boss to terminate your employment.

The practice of doing your best refers to consistently striving for a high level of performance, putting forth a maximum effort, and aiming for exceptional outcomes in what you do. Having a mindset of pursuing excellence drives personal growth and professional success.

> *"The greatest day in your life and mine is*
> *when we take total responsibility for our attitudes.*
> *That's the day we truly grow up."*
> John C. Maxwell

PRACTICAL TIPS

Cultivating positive attitudes can greatly impact your life and those around you. Here are some simple and easy-to-implement tips to help you embrace a positive attitude:

Smile: A smile can light up a room. It will make others feel welcome and appreciated.

Be grateful: Regularly acknowledge and express gratitude for the blessings in your life.

Be kind: Treat others with kindness and compassion. Remember that others are facing their own battles.

Be positive: Speak positively, avoid gossip, and don't complain or grumble. Focus on solutions, not on who to blame.

Be Complimentary: Sincerely compliment others on their work and achievements.

Encourage others: Be a cheerleader and motivator for others.

Be enthusiastic: Let your excitement and passion for things you enjoy be contagious.

Forgive: Do not hold grudges and resentments. Focus on moving forward positively.

Celebrate: Appreciate your achievements and those of others.

IMPORTANCE TO AN EMPLOYER

Employers highly value employees with positive attitudes. Such employees bring benefits to the workplace, producing a more harmonious environment. The employee who radiates optimism and enthusiasm can uplift an entire team, motivating others to perform at their best. This creates a work environment where collaboration and teamwork thrive.

Individuals with a positive attitude tend to handle challenges and setbacks more effectively. They approach obstacles with a can-do mindset and seek solutions rather than dwell on problems. This resilience not only makes them valuable problem-solvers but also helps the company navigate tough times more easily.

Positive employees are generally more adaptable to change. In today's fast-paced and ever-evolving business landscape, adaptability is very important. Such individuals are open to learning new skills, embracing innovation, and adjusting to shifting priorities. This makes them valuable assets to employers.

In customer-contact roles, employees with uplifting attitudes produce positive impressions on clients and customers. Their genuine warmth and empathy lead to improved customer satisfaction and loyalty.

Positive attitudes are also closely linked to higher levels of creativity and innovation. Such employees inspire and motivate their colleagues to creative solutions. They become catalysts for positive change within the organization.

Employees who embrace a positive attitude fosters a supportive work culture. Such individuals significantly contribute to the overall success and well-being of the organization.[0]

> *"Virtually nothing is impossible in this world if you just put your mind to it and maintain a positive attitude."*
> Lou Holtz

EXAMPLES: Positive Attitude Core Value Statements.

Here are sample core value statements that you might choose if you were going to adopt a positive attitude as a personal core value:

1. I choose to be positive and uplift others through my words and actions.

2. I believe in the power of a positive attitude to transform challenges into opportunities.

3. I commit to approaching every situation with optimism and enthusiasm.

4. I will strive to be a source of inspiration and encouragement to those around me through my personal attitudes.

5. I choose to see the good in people and situations, fostering a positive outlook.

6. I value a supportive environment for my family and friends.

7. I maintain a positive outlook even in the face of adversity.

8. I choose to be a positive role model and mentor for others. I will lead by example.

MY PERSONAL CORE VALUE – Positive and Uplifting Attitude

Adopt or confirm your core value. If a positive and uplifting attitude is already a core value, or if you want to establish it as a core value, write your personal core value in the space below. You may want to use the examples above as guides to draft your Personal Core Value Statement. Make it short, succinct, and meaningful to you. Something you can easily remember.

Positive Attitude:

_____
_____
_____
_____
_____
_____
_____
_____

DISCUSSION AND THOUGHT QUESTIONS

1. Share some personal experiences that demonstrate the power of positive and uplifting attitudes in your life.

2. How would you define an uplifting attitude? What are the most important characteristics associated with having a positive attitude?

3. Why do you think a positive attitude is considered a valuable personal core value?

4. What are some practical ways in which individuals can cultivate a positive and uplifting attitude, especially during challenging times?

5. Reflect on a time when you faced a difficult situation. How did your attitude affect your perception of the challenge and your ability to overcome it?

6. How do positive and uplifting attitudes influence your relationships with others? Give examples of how such attitudes have improved interpersonal connections or resolved conflicts.

7. What role do positive attitudes play in fostering resilience and overcoming challenges? Share stories of individuals who have demonstrated resilience through their positive mindsets.

8. How does having a positive and uplifting attitude impact one's mental and emotional well-being?

9. Think of public figures or role models who embody positive and uplifting attitudes. Or negative attitudes? What can we learn from their examples?

10. Discuss the ripple effect of being positive. How can one person's positive attitude inspire others in their work, social circles, or community?

NOTES

<u>I want to do the following:</u>

a. _____

b. _____

c. _____

d. _____

<u>I want to remember:</u>

a. _____

b. _____

c. _____

d. _____

Action Challenge: Identify a negative thought pattern that tends to dominate your thinking. Challenge that pattern by consciously reframing your thoughts in a more positive light. Practice this exercise daily, and observe how it impacts your mood, resilience, and overall well-being.

Free PDF
MAKE WISE DECISIONS
[Get the ebook version for 99 cents]

Consequences Shape Lives.

This book discusses the nature of decisions and explores eight essential questions to make better decisions.

You are a few decisions away from transforming your life. You can make better decisions! This resource has sections on what makes a poor decision, questions to ask yourself, traps to avoid, short and sweet decisions, the wise decision framework, and twenty ways to be wise. It also has a handy decision-making checklist. (12 pages)

Free PDF: https://getwisdompublishing.com/resource-registration/

Kindle ebook for 99 cents: https://www.amazon.com/dp/B0FG8NC53J

Ebook

Free PDF

Ten Steps to Wise Choices

Timeless Wisdom. Practical Tools. Lasting Impact.

Free PDF
Life Improvement Principles
[Get the ebook version for 99 cents]

You can live your best life!

Welcome to a journey of discovery! In case you have forgotten, your actions have consequences. Unlock your potential! This book (60+ pages) provides the overview of all our strategies and wisdom principles to live your best life. You *can* transform your life! Get your wisdom-based roadmap to a better life and unlock all the possibilities for growth and success.

Free PDF: https://getwisdompublishing.com/resource-registration/

Kindle ebook for 99 cents:
https://www.amazon.com/dp/B0FG883KZM

Ebook

Free PDF

Make it your life goal to be the best you can be!

Discover Wisdom and live the life you deserve.

Next Steps - Implementation

What should you do next? Your first task should be to finalize the core values for your life by adopting four to six values. Obviously choose the number you are comfortable with.

Some of the core values we've discussed are probably already present in your life. Celebrate those! At the same time, perhaps you've realized that there are some additional core values you should adopt. You may also have some behaviors or habits that conflict with these core values and hopefully some that support them. The logical next step would be to work at correcting any negative behavior and begin to establish positive habits that will cement new behaviors into your everyday life.

Our suggestion is that you complete the following Worksheet for each core value you have chosen.

Core Value Worksheet

Core Value Statement:
Enter the Core Value Statement that you have chosen for yourself.

_____

_____

_____

Actions to stop or change:

A. List any habits or behaviors you possess that are in conflict with this core value.

1. _____
2. _____
3. _____
4. _____
5. _____

B. Resolve to stop or change these behaviors. Choose one that is particularly troubling and list it below and physically write out what you are <u>not</u> going to do: _____

_____

_____

_____

_____

After one or two weeks, choose another one that you want to focus on, etc.

Actions to undertake:

A. For this core value review the "Practical Tips" section in the chapter and choose <u>several</u> tips you would like to begin implementing:

1. Action: _____

_____

2. Action: _____

_____

3. Action: _____

_____

4. Action: _____

_____

B. Chose one and intentionally begin to practice the behavior. When appropriate choose another one, etc.

C. After you are comfortable with the easier tips, consider choosing a more involved or difficult behavior that was suggested in the chapter.

Transformation Roadmap
Core Values That Will Transform Your Life!

1. Living with **honesty, integrity, and truth** creates a solid foundation for personal growth, success, and meaningful relationships. These traits foster trust, reliability, and a life free from the stress and chaos of deceit.

2. Being **trustworthy** creates respect, reliability, and meaningful connections with others.

3. Being **humble** allows you to acknowledge your limitations, accept constructive feedback. It allows you to practice empathy, respect, and open communication, allowing more meaningful connections.

4. **Forgiveness** is a decision that allows you to release yourself from the burden of grudges, revenge, and emotional stress. It also permits you to move forward with your life.

5. Embracing **accountability** means taking responsibility for your actions and decisions, allowing you to learn from mistakes, avoid excuses, and actively shape your personal and professional success.

6. Know and honor yourself. **Authenticity** is being consistent with your core values and beliefs, ensuring you make choices that reflect your true self rather than conforming to external pressures.

7. Being **genuine** and honest with yourself and others fosters trust and deeper connections, allowing you to build more meaningful relationships.

8. Expressing **gratitude** fosters stronger connections and enhances emotional support, making life more fulfilling and joyful. Gratitude and thankfulness help maintain inner peace and optimism.

9. Acts of **generosity** improve mental and physical health and increase feelings of purpose and satisfaction.

10. **Kindness** enhances your personal well-being. Practicing kindness improves your mental health and fosters a sense of calmness in life.

11. Practicing **compassion** fosters stronger connections and enhances personal well-being by creating a more supportive and understanding environment within your sphere of influence.

12. Striving for **equality** allows individuals to pursue paths that align with their unique skills and passions, leading to greater personal happiness and societal satisfaction. It ensures that people receive the resources they need based on their specific circumstances, fostering a healthier, more just society where everyone can thrive.

13. Developing **self-awareness** through personal growth allows you to understand your strengths and weaknesses, enabling more informed decisions and a clearer sense of purpose in life. It also enhances resilience and self-confidence, empowering you to face challenges and take control of your life with a positive mindset.

14. **Diligence** provides a foundation for a meaningful work. Consistently applying focused effort and self-discipline helps align daily actions with long-term goals, leading to a more fulfilling personal and work life. It requires prioritizing important tasks, and persevering through challenges.

15. **Honor** means you consistently align your actions with values such as integrity, courage, and selflessness, fostering a deep sense of self-respect and purpose in life. Treating others with dignity and thoughtfulness creates mutual trust, improves your relationships, and contributes to a harmonious environment.

16. **Justice** rooted in fairness and respect improves mental health and the quality of life, fostering trust and satisfaction in the community.

17. Maintaining a **positive attitude** helps you navigate challenges with resilience and promotes reduced stress and a more gentle community. It will foster better relationships and encourage proactive behaviors that lead to personal and professional success.

Your decisions shape your life.
Start building with intention!

What About Other Books in the Series?

Change Your Life with purpose and intention!

Should you read other books in this series?

We recommend that if you acquire any books in the Series, you should also obtain *CHOOSE Integrity*. This is the foundational book in the series. We also believe the four books covering the Primary Life Principles would be particularly useful for living a better life: Friends, Speech, Diligence (Work), and Money.

CHOOSE Faith

This is a unique book in the Series. It addresses all the important spiritual type questions you might consider. It answers questions like: Does God exist? Why should I care about faith? What's religion all about? Does eternal life really exist? I don't know the right questions to ask. What is the truth? This book will help you find answers to your spiritual questions.

LIFE PLANNING HANDBOOK

This book is also unique. If you are interested in doing a complete life plan that covers all aspects of your life, not just a specific topic like those addressed in The Life Planning Series, go to:

https://www.amazon.com/dp/1952359325

You can live a better life.
Just Decide You Want to!

The Life Planning Series

These books can improve your life.

LIFE PLANNING HANDBOOK	**A Life Plan will shape your life journey!** The next step in your life planning.
CHOOSE INTEGRITY	**Life Principle:** Be honest, live with integrity, and base your life on truth.
CHOOSE FRIENDS WISELY	**Life Principle:** Choose your friends wisely.
CHOOSE THE RIGHT WORDS	**Life Principle:** Guard your speech.
CHOOSE GOOD WORK HABITS	**Life Principle:** Be diligent and a hard worker.
CHOOSE FINANCIAL RESPONSIBILITY	**Life Principle:** Make sound financial choices.

CHOOSE A POSITIVE SELF-IMAGE	**Life Principle:** Be confident in who you are.
CHOOSE LEADERSHIP	**Life Principle:** Lead well and be a loyal follower.
CHOOSE CORE VALUES	**Life Principle:** Core values will drive your life.
CHOOSE LOVE AND FAMILY	**Life Principle:** Build strong relationships.
CHOOSE FAITH	*Your Spiritual Guidebook for Questions about Religion, God, Heaven, Truth, Evil, and the Afterlife.*

Go to: **https://www.amazon.com/dp/B09TH9SYC4**

to get your copy.

Create a life based on purpose, meaning, and lasting fulfillment.

Notes

QUOTES

ACCURACY: We have used a number of quotes throughout this book that came from our files, notes, books, public articles, the Internet, etc. We have made no attempt to verify that these quotes were actually written or spoken by the person they are attributed to. Regardless of the source of these quotes, the wisdom of the underlying message is relative to the content in this book and worth noting, even if the source reference is erroneous.

SOURCE: Unless otherwise specifically noted below the quotes used herein can be sourced from a number of different websites on the Internet that provide lists of quotes by subject or author. The same or similar quotes will appear on multiple sites. Therefore, rather than assign individual quote sources, we are providing a list of sites where we might have found the quotes that were used in this book:

--azquotes.com
--codeofliving.com
--goodhousekeeping.com
--graciousquotes.com
--keepinspiring.me
--parade.com
--quotemaster.org
--success.com
--thoughtcatalog.com
--wisesayings.com

--brainyquote.com
--everydaypower.com
--goodreads.com/quotes
--inc.com
--notable-quotes.com
--plantetofsuccess.com
--quotir.com
--thoughtco.com
--wisdomquotes.com
--wow4u.com

0 This section, "Importance To An Employer," in each chapter was initially produced by an AI tool (ChatGPT, Bing, or BARD) and then rewritten and edited to be consistent with the views of the author.

1 This illustration is fictional and was produced by an AI tool (ChatGPT, Bing, or BARD) for the purpose of illustrating the concept and nature of the subject core value. The AI material was rewritten and edited to ensure that it was consistent with the views of the author.

2 Search for "Mary Johnson and Oshea Israel" on the internet, this story appears on hundreds of sites.

3 *Unbelievable And True Inspiring Stories of Mercy - Mindsetopia.* https://mindsetopia.com/inspiring-stories-of-mercy/.

4 Sharon Stonestreet, sermoncentral.com, Sept 8, 2007.

5 Lysa Terkeurst, *The Best Yes,* Thomas Nelson Publisher, ISBN: 978-1-4002-02585-1.

Resources and Bibliography

1 Values First: How Knowing Your Core Beliefs Can Get You the Life and Career You Want Paperback, Laura Eigel, Houndstooth Press (April 6, 2022), ISBN: 978-1544528830.

2 Discovering Your Authentic Core Values: A step-by-step guide Paperback, Marc Alan Schelske, Live210 Media (December 11, 2012), ISBN: 978-0988688209.

3 The Values Factor: The Secret to Creating an Inspired and Fulfilling Life Paperback, John F. Demartini, Berkley, 1st edition (October 1, 2013), ISBN: 978-0425264744.

4 Jennifer Herrity, "14 Essential Leadership Values To Consider Developing, Indeed.com, updated Feb 28 2023.

5 The Core Value Equation: A Framework to Drive Results, Create Limitless Scale and Win the War for Talent Hardcover, Darius Mirshahzadeh, Lioncrest Publishing (April 27, 2020), ISBN: 978-1544506722.

6 The Live Your Values Deck: Sort Out, Honor, and Practice What Matters Most to You Cards, Lisa Congdon and Andrees Niculescu, Chronicle Books (November 9, 2021), ISBN: 978-1797206127.

7 A Book of Values: Your Personal Guide to Meaning and Happiness, Alan Kovitz, Elevations Unlimited (November 2, 2021), ISBN: 978-1990093326.

8 The Attributes: 25 Hidden Drivers of Optimal Performance Hardcover, Rich Diviney, Random House (January 26, 2021), ISBN: 978-0593133941.

9 The Road to Character, David Brooks, Random House (September 13, 2016), ISBN: 978-0812983418.

10 Character is Destiny: The Value of Personal Ethics in Everyday Life Paperback, Russell W. Gough, Living Book Press (February 11, 2020), ISBN: 978-1922348081.

11 The Power of Character in Leadership: How Values, Morals, Ethics, and Principles Affect Leaders, Myles Munroe, Whitaker House, ISBN: 978-1629119496.

12 Proving the Value of Leadership Development: Case Studies from Top Leadership Development Programs, Ph.D. Jack J. Phillips, Ph.D. Patti P. Phillips, Ph.D. Rebecca Ray, Hope Nicholas, Panther Publishing (January 1, 2023), ISBN: 978-0980216950.

About the Author

The author graduated from the Business School at Indiana University and obtained a master's degree at Georgia State University in Atlanta. His first career was as a senior executive with a top insurance and financial institution, where he spent a number of years directing strategic planning for one of their major divisions.

In the 1990s he founded an online Internet business which he sold in 2010. He began to write and publish books and materials that led to an interest in personal life planning. This resulted in combining the wisdom of wise sayings and proverbs with life planning and the result is the Life Planning Series and the Life Planning Handbook.

The author, his wife, and two of his children and their families live in the Nashville, TN area.

WEBSITE: http://www.lifeplanningtools.com

AMAZON: www.amazon.com/author/jswellman

Contact Us

	www.lifeplanningtools.com info@lifeplanningtools.com	Website Email
Facebook	JSWellman	
	www.amazon.com/author/jswellman	**Author Page**
Life Planning Series	www.amazon.com/dp/B09TH9SYC4	
	www.lifeplanningtools.link/newsletter	**Monthly News Letter**

You can help

IDEAS and SUGGESTIONS: If you have a suggestion to improve this book, please let us know.

Mention our LIFE PLANNING books on your social platforms and recommend them to your family and friends.

Thank you!

Make a Difference

"The law of prosperity is generosity.
If you want more, give more."
Bob Proctor[57]

Have you ever done something just out of kindness or goodwill without wanting or expecting anything in return? I'm going to ask you to do <u>two things</u> just for that reason. The first will be just out of the goodness of your heart and the second to make an impact in someone else's life.

It won't cost you anything and it won't take a lot of time or effort.

This Book

First, what did you think of this book? Give the book an honest review in order for us to compete with the giant publishers. What did you like and how did it impact you? It will only take you several minutes to leave your review at:
https://www.amazon.com/dp/195235949X

Follow the link above to the Amazon sales page, scroll down about three quarters of the page and click the box that says: "Write a customer review." It does not have to be long or well-written – just tell other readers what you think about the book. Or, just score the book on a scale of 1 – 5 stars (5 is high).

This will help us a great deal and we so appreciate your willingness to help. If you want to tell us something about the book directly, you can email us at: info@lifeplanningtools.com.

Give Books to Students and Employees

Secondly, do you know any schools or organizations that might want to give this book or our Life Planning Handbook to their students or emloyees?

Here is how you can help. If you send us the contact information and allow us to use your name, we will contact the person or persons you suggest with all the details. Obviously there would be special pricing and if the order is large enough, a message from the organization's CEO could be included on the printed pages.

Alternatively, you can personally give a copy of one of our books to the organization for their consideration. We would recommend our Life Planning Handbook, but some organizations might be interested in a specific subject. If they are interested in this partnership with us, they should contact us directly.

It is not that difficult to help someone live a better life: just a little time and intentionality. Let us hear from you if you want to make a difference in someone's life!

J. S. Wellman
Extra-mile Publishing
steve@lifeplanningtools.com
www.lifeplanningtools.com

Wisdom Without Action is Just information!

www.ingramcontent.com/pod-product-compliance
Lightning Source LLC
Chambersburg PA
CBHW070114070426
42448CB00039B/2713